ROLLS-ROYCE ARMOURED CAR

1915–44 (all models)

First published in March 2017

David Fletcher has asserted his moral right to
be identified as the author of this work.

A catalogue record for this book is available
from the British Library.

ISBN 978 1 78521 058 7

Library of Congress control no. 2016917313

Published by Haynes Publishing,
Sparkford, Yeovil,
Somerset BA22 7JJ, UK.
Tel: 01963 440635
Int. tel: +44 1963 440635
Website: www.haynes.com

Haynes North America Inc.,
861 Lawrence Drive, Newbury Park,
California 91320, USA.

Printed in Malaysia.

Copy editor: Michelle Tilling
Proof reader: Penny Housden
Indexer: Peter Nicholson
Page design: James Robertson

ROLLS-ROYCE ARMOURED CAR

1915–44 (all models)

Owners' Workshop Manual

An insight into the design, construction and operation of the legendary armoured patrol vehicle in two world wars

David Fletcher MBE

With additional material from Captain Stephen Mac Eoin (Military Archives, Defence Forces Ireland) and James Black (James Black Restorations Ltd); and Ian Hudson (Research Assistant), Steve Latham (Workshop volunteer), Matt Sampson (Photographer) and David Willey (Curator) of the Tank Museum, Bovington, England.

Contents

OPPOSITE The 40/50hp Rolls-Royce six-cylinder, water-cooled engine.

Introduction

The Rolls-Royce armoured car has a particular cachet at the Tank Museum. We are fortunate to own one of only two original complete and running examples remaining, the Irish Army Collection at The Curragh has the second. Is its special appeal because it is a Rolls-Royce? Something about that name and a period that immediately brings visions of style, quality, Empire, 'the best' – or is it the associations with the First World War, serving in far-flung outposts with names like Lawrence of Arabia?

The Tank Museum vehicle has a well-recorded history and in places it bears the scars to show for its travels and service. Some well-meaning Silver Ghost owners once suggested having the fenders straightened or replaced – a Rolls-Royce surely should look like a well-presented Rolls-Royce. The suggestion was politely declined. The dented fenders are part not just of the vehicle's history – something we at the museum are obviously keen to see

preserved – but they also add to the vehicle's character, and this brings us back to the word cachet. Some vehicles do seem to have a character, an aura, some essence that others simply do not have. It is true in other fields of mechanical engineering – an item that rises above the rest to act as an icon, having not just engineering excellence but the flavour of a period, an identification with the zeitgeist; such as the Flying Scotsman, the Mini or the Spitfire. The Rolls-Royce armoured car, with its stately presence, has this essence by the bucketload.

The vehicle has been understandably held in high regard by staff at the museum. It has always been a runner and has carried HM the Queen at parades, led her down Pall Mall and performed faultlessly at Royal Tournaments, Standard presentations, regimental amalgamations and museum displays over the decades. The late, lamented Chatty Taylor, Workshop Foreman at the Tank Museum and teller of amazing tales in a rich language, guarded and cosseted the

BELOW A dramatic watercolour showing what was hoped Rolls-Royce armoured cars might be capable of in action.
(6559-101_E1996.2047)

ABOVE **The Tank Museum's car displays its original Army census number, M247, with the prefix 'M' denoting 'Motor Car'. This was changed to F247 in the mid-1920s when armoured cars were given the prefix 'F'.**

Rolls at a great number of these events – including taking the car to the 1997 Concours Automobiles Classiques in Paris. One of Chatty's great delights was starting the engine – then asking how many people knew the car was running – such was the silence of the famous six-cylinder engine. A *Daily Telegraph* journalist wrote of his experience of being taken for a drive in the car: 'I noticed a discreet signal from Chatty; I got down and looked at the speedometer as bidden. Good grief, the engine seemed to be just ticking over. He looked over his shoulder and grinned.'

In this book another stalwart of the Tank Museum staff – David Fletcher MBE – uses his extensive knowledge and original writing style to tell of the history and use of the Rolls-Royce armoured car. Here are stories of campaigns few of us will have heard of – as well as tales of the car in better-known actions. David has sourced an amazing range of images on the subject from the Tank Museum's Archives and other sources – many of which have not been

published before. And of course there are plenty of new images of the museum's own vehicle to delight enthusiast, layman, and model-maker alike. David's own long familiarity with this particular vehicle and his affection for the type comes across in the writing and this book adds another volume to his extensive contribution to the history of armoured vehicles.

The history and restoration of *Sliabh na MBan*, the Irish Defence Forces Rolls-Royce armoured car, adds another dimension to the book and our thanks go to Captain Stephen Mac Eoin of the Military Archives of Defence Forces Ireland, and James Black of James Black Restorations Ltd for their contributions.

David Willey
Curator, Tank Museum

Chapter One

Mr Rolls and Mr Royce

'Strive for perfection in everything you do. Take the best that exists and make it better. When it does not exist, design it.'

Sir Henry Royce

OPPOSITE For all its mechanical sophistication, it is always worth remembering that, as with all military vehicles, the most important element of any Rolls-Royce was its crew.

The War Office Mechanical Transport Committee was charged, among its duties, with attending the annual Motor Car Exhibition at Olympia every November, to keep an eye on British motor car production and form some idea of what was going on in the trade. In 1906 they were required to make a list of all low-powered British-made cars selling for £450 or less that they considered suitable for military use. From among these they selected a 10hp Wolseley-Siddeley at £300, although they were very taken with a 20hp Royce which was of remarkable quality but too expensive – at £525 for the chassis only – marketed by C.S. Rolls and Co.

The Honourable Charles Rolls and Henry Royce had met by this time and formed the Rolls-Royce Company. Their badge of the letter R duplicated and overlapping was already in use on the radiators of their cars and was becoming established. But as yet the two men were not working together. Frederick Henry Royce (to give his full name) was a gifted engineer; he started out delivering newspapers and then worked as a telegraph boy, but an apprenticeship with the Great Northern Railway in Peterborough set him on his way. By 1884, with what money he had and more from a dedicated friend, he started his own business in Cooke Street, Manchester. Royce did not consider himself inventive, but with his well-honed engineering skills, dedication and sheer hard work, he developed the knack of improving machines until they reached his standards of perfection, starting to specialise in dynamos and electric cranes. A Royce product was quieter, smoother, more reliable and longer-lasting than its rivals, and on such a basis business grew until the partners could afford houses, start families and even invest in early motor cars. Royce settled for a second-hand 10hp Decauville, a two-cylinder car with a four-speed gearbox, noted for its reliability. With the Decauville to experiment on, Royce took advantage of a lull in the crane business to begin manufacturing his own cars. Three

OPPOSITE **Charles Stewart Rolls.** *(The Granger Collection/ TopFoto)*

BELOW **Sir Henry Royce.** *(Public domain)*

two-cylinder 10hp machines were built, and
although Royce was obliged to buy in many
components which could not be made in
Cooke Street, he insisted upon the highest
standards so that when the first one was
completed it ran at once without a breakdown.

The Honourable Charles Stewart Rolls was the
third son of Lord Llangattock of Monmouthshire;
he was at Cambridge, studying engineering,
when he developed a passionate interest in the
Continental pursuit of motoring and soon became
quite an expert in the engineering aspects.
So much so, in fact, that he soon became an
acknowledged expert in the subject and was also
dabbling in aviation – specifically in balloons and
heavier-than-air machines. From 1903 Rolls set
up in business as a car dealer and the following
year persuaded Claude Goodman Johnson to
join him in partnership. By 1905, he was trading
as C.S. Rolls and Company from premises
in Conduit Street, selling mostly top-quality
Continental cars to discerning British motorists
with plenty of money.

Of the three original cars built by Henry
Royce, the third one went to Henry Edmunds,
a director of Royce's company, and it was
Edmunds who engineered a meeting between
Rolls and Royce. The meeting took place at the
Grand Central Hotel in Manchester. After test
driving the car, Charles Rolls realised that here

was a machine of superior quality and agreed
to take all the cars that Royce could make,
adopting the classic radiator and the name
Rolls-Royce at the same time.

By late 1906 new land was acquired in Derby
for an enlarged factory and the company, Rolls-
Royce Ltd, was formed with Royce as Chief
Engineer and Works Director and Charles Rolls
as Technical Managing Director, at the head.
That year also saw the introduction of the new
six-cylinder 40/50hp design from which Claude
Johnson took the thirteenth chassis, fitted it with
a touring car body and had it painted with silver
aluminium paint. Embellished with silver-plated
lights and other fittings and carrying the name
Silver Ghost on a cast plate, it was entered in a
series of long-distance trial runs watched closely
by inspectors from the Royal Automobile Club.
All these it passed with flying colours, doing
more than double the distance of its closest
rival. Consequently, the name Silver Ghost has
since been adopted almost as a model name
for this type of car, although at the outset it
only applied to a specific vehicle. It was Claude
Johnson, the Commercial Managing Director,
who persuaded his fellow directors to drop
the smaller cars in the range and go for a one-
model policy. They were not all in agreement
but, being unable to match Johnson's superb
business acumen, had to agree in the end. So

the 40/50hp six-cylinder car, ultimately known as the Silver Ghost, was in full production from 1907 until 1925, encompassing all the years of the First World War. There were modifications of course, virtually year by year and often different series within the year, but they were all essentially Silver Ghosts.

Charles Rolls is reckoned to have been the first Briton to be killed in an air crash, when his Wright biplane broke up during an airshow at Hengistbury near Bournemouth on 11 July 1910. He was only at about 20ft and in the process of landing when the accident happened, but was killed almost instantly. He had already resigned as Technical Managing Director of Rolls-Royce Ltd to concentrate on flying, although he had been retained as Technical Adviser.

Henry Royce died in 1933, having been ill off and on since 1911. It was due in part to working all hours and grabbing food (when he remembered) in passing. Latterly he spent his winters in the south of France, although he always kept work at the forefront of his mind and always had at least one project on the go wherever he was.

The six-cylinder engine already existed when Rolls-Royce was founded, the 40/50hp unit was not the first by any means, but it was the quietest and most reliable due to intense concentration on detail. The block was cast as two groups of three cylinders with a collective capacity of 7,428cc in 1909 with a dual ignition system (two plugs per cylinder), one high tension with trembler coil, the other through a high-tension magneto driven off the crankshaft. This was the heart of the Silver Ghost linked to a three-speed (1909 only) or four-speed transmission with a cone clutch and driving the rear axle through a final drive, the ratio of which changed over the years.

A pedal-operated brake worked on the propeller shaft, while the handbrake acted on the rear wheels. Front-wheel brakes were not introduced until 1924. The suspension comprised semi-elliptical springs all round; cantilevered rear springs were introduced in 1911 and were standardised in 1912. Wooden-spoked artillery-pattern wheels were usual to begin with, but wire-spoked wheels, having been available as an option, became the standard type in 1913, although artillery wheels were available until 1921. There were different chassis lengths and wheelbases available at different times, ranging from 180in (135.5in wheelbase) in 1907 to 196.75in (150.5in wheelbase) in 1923.

The total number of Silver Ghosts produced was 6,173, along with a further 1,703 in the United States – the renowned but expensive Springfield Silver Ghosts.

BELOW The Rolls-Royce Silver Ghost 1907 Scottish reliability trials. *(TopFoto)*

Chapter Two

The First World War

—(●)—

'A Rolls in the desert was above rubies. . . . Great was Rolls and great was Royce! They were worth hundreds of men to us in those deserts.'

T.E. Lawrence

OPPOSITE A Rolls-Royce armoured car salvaging a British Martinsyde aeroplane, which was captured from German Turkish aerodrome at Tekrit, Iraq, 1918. *(TopFoto)*

ABOVE **A turreted Silver Ghost in Royal Navy service outside the Clement Talbot Works in Barlby Road, North Kensington, which at that time was also the headquarters of the Royal Naval Armoured Car Division.**

With the Royal Navy

On Sunday 15 November 1914 the first turreted Rolls-Royce armoured car arrived in London. It had been driven all the way down from Glasgow and was heading for what would be the Royal Naval Armoured Car Division's headquarters in Barlby Road, North Kensington, probably better known as the Clement Talbot Motor Works. Six more cars turned up by 10 December and they continued to arrive in a steady stream from then on.

William Beardmore and Company of Glasgow developed the armour for the cars. It

LEFT **In this head-on view of a car in the same location the visor in front of the driver is closed so he only has a narrow slit to look out of. Also of note are the front tyres (and the spares), which are of different patterns. At the time this was believed to reduce the risk of skidding.**

was 8mm-thick nickel chrome steel and their Mr Scott is credited with devising a means of bending the plate without cracking it to form the circular turret and curved fighting compartment.

However, these were not the very first Rolls-Royce armoured cars. For those we need to go back to the first days of the war and introduce Commander Charles Rumney Samson, a Royal Navy officer and probably the first Briton to use armoured cars in war. We don't have a precise date for the first car, but somewhere around September or October 1914 seems likely. Nor was it armoured in the proper sense. Rather, it was fitted with panels of 6mm steel plate by the Dunkirk shipyard Forges et Chantiers de France to a design worked out by Felix Samson, Charles Samson's brother. It started life as a Rolls-Royce 40/50hp touring car, part of the fleet operated by the Eastchurch Squadron Royal Naval Air Service that Charles Samson commanded in Flanders. It may well have been one of the pilots' private cars. Steel panels covered the sides, raised up at the back for added protection and mounting a water-cooled Maxim machine-gun which could be fired over the back. Steel was also used instead of a windscreen to protect the driver and at the very front to enclose the classic radiator with a panel to regulate airflow. However, tests revealed that

ABOVE Charles Samson's original Rolls-Royce with improvised 6mm boilerplate armour and mounting a Maxim machine-gun, in the Dunkirk shipyard of Forges et Chantiers de France, where it was put together.

BELOW This is another view of the same car with some Royal Navy riflemen, but in this case it is armed with a Lewis machine-gun.

ABOVE First Admiralty-pattern Rolls-Royce armoured car at Dunkirk in October 1914. The officer on the left is Flight Lieutenant Reggie Marix of the Royal Naval Air Service (RNAS), one of Charles Samson's pilots. On 8 October 1914 he was one of three Sopwith Tabloid pilots who bombed the Zeppelin sheds at Düsseldorf, destroying the first Zeppelin of the war.

RIGHT A wooden mock-up of a First Admiralty-pattern armoured car on a genuine Rolls-Royce Silver Ghost chassis, to a design conceived by Lord Wimborne and a Mr Macnamara of the Admiralty.

the steel was vulnerable to rifle bullets at any range under 500yd.

At the same time the Admiralty Air Department in London initiated the construction of 60 armoured cars, at the request of Charles Samson and on the authority of Winston Churchill, First Lord of the Admiralty. These cars featured proper armour plate of nickel chrome steel, albeit only 4mm thick but backed on the inside of the crew compartment with oak planks. The protective armour was no higher than the bonnet of the car. For some reason Samson was not consulted although

a mock-up of the design was built on a Rolls-Royce chassis and approved by Churchill. Two individuals at the Admiralty – Lord Wimborne and a Mr Macnamara – drew up the design, of which 60 were ordered, 18 of them on Rolls-Royce chassis. Samson and his men did not like the Admiralty cars since, apart from the driver, other members of the crew were exposed to enemy fire unless they laid flat behind the armour, and even then they could be hit by rifle fire from first-floor windows as the cars were entirely open at the top. Samson modified one of the Rolls-Royces in France by

ABOVE Photographed on the Menin Road in Belgium near what came to be known as Hellfire Corner, this is possibly the same First Admiralty-pattern Rolls-Royce surrounded by an admiring group of Guards officers.

RIGHT A modification on a First Admiralty-pattern Rolls-Royce devised by Charles Samson and fabricated at the Forges et Chantiers de France shipyard in Dunkirk, possibly from real armour plate supplied by the Admiralty in London. It is towing a 47mm (3pdr) gun on an improvised carriage.

LEFT In another view of Samson's improved First Admiralty-pattern Rolls-Royce, it can be seen how the armour was built up around the crew compartment, and what appear to be double opening flaps on the back.

ABOVE This is possibly the first turreted Rolls-Royce, but this time it is not for the Royal Navy. It was armoured on a Silver Ghost chassis by the London coachbuilders Barker & Co. for the Scottish Horse (a Yeomanry regiment), more or less as a private deal, since at that time (in late 1914) the War Office was not interested.

extending the armour upwards and sloping it inwards to provide more protection for the crew, and this car was often seen towing a 47mm (3-pounder) gun on an improvised two-wheeled carriage. Later on, this particular vehicle seems to have gone out to the Mediterranean, although the fate of the others is not clear. The gradual extension of the trench system was inhibiting their use and with the arrival of the turreted cars they quickly faded from the scene. None of them were ever seen again, unless of course some of the chassis were rebuilt as turreted cars. Samson himself said that 'Rolls-Royces proved by far the most reliable and suitable.' He was learning fast.

In all, an estimated 89 turreted Rolls-Royce armoured cars were built, the chassis being either newly built or withdrawn from dealers: there is no evidence of any armoured cars being built on chassis donated by private individuals. The cars were divided between seven squadrons of the Royal Naval Armoured Car Division, 1, 2, 3, 4, 7 and 8 Squadrons were issued with twelve cars each, a further six went to No 14 Squadron and two cars are believed to have accompanied the Russian Armoured Car Division. The remaining nine cars seem to have been retained as spares or for experimental purposes. The other squadrons – there were 18 in all to begin with – had either Lanchester armoured cars (5, 6 and

15 Squadrons), motorcycle combinations (9, 10, 11,12 and 13 Squadrons), or Seabrook armoured lorries (six each in 16, 17 and 18 Squadrons). The Rolls-Royce squadrons, however, are the only ones that interest us here.

At least two major differences have been noted between cars built at this time. The side plates reaching from the front part of the fighting compartment to the rear of the engine are either in two pieces connected by rivets in line with the driver's visor or from a single panel, slightly bent at about the same place. Furthermore, the area in front of the driver's visor is either made from three flat panels riveted together or formed from a single panel curved to fit. We are unable to explain this, although it may be due to where the hulls were assembled in London. Barker & Co. of South Audley Street has been suggested while the J.E. Thomas Auto Coachbuilding Company, which went into liquidation in 1916, has also been mentioned. There may well have been others. Armoured hulls in kit form are believed to have been sent down from Glasgow by William Beardmore and Company where the armour had been made. Other firms may also have been involved.

The secret of the Silver Ghost's success was essentially a result of the strength of the chassis. This was formed from two massive side girders connected crosswise by five strong pieces that acted as cross members. It was powered by a water-cooled six-cylinder petrol engine, in two blocks of three, rated at 7,428cc. This drove through a cone clutch to a four-speed and reverse gearbox and from there by shaft to the rear axle. Semi-elliptical leaf springs at the front supported the front axle, while at the rear they were cantilevered out to provide extra springing and were strengthened to support the heavy armoured body. A crank handle at the front was used for starting, but since this required the driver to dismount, which could be risky under fire, an internal starting device, working off the flywheel, was invented by Petty Officer A.E. Coyne and installed in most cars. Since the Rolls-Royce had dual ignition, a warm engine could sometimes be restarted by using the magneto and a trembler coil to initiate a spark. There were no brakes acting on the front wheels at all, as was normal in those days. The handbrake acted on the rear wheels while the footbrake pedal acted on the prop shaft. Since all armoured car chassis had to be prepared at the Derby works (with extra-strong springs, twin rear wheels and relocated fuel and lubrication tanks), armoured cars could not normally be built using donated vehicles, except in special cases. Armour plate was created from nickel chrome steel by William Beardmore and Company of Glasgow and supplied in kit form to Barker & Co., coachbuilders of South Audley Street, London, where they were assembled as armoured cars.

Most of the squadrons, as they formed, were sent to do a bit of shakedown training, usually in East Anglia, which was perceived to be under threat from German invasion. The first of these to become operational and go overseas was No 2 Squadron, commanded by His Grace the Second Duke of Westminster. It comprised the usual 12 turreted Rolls-Royce armoured cars and 3 of the new Seabrook armoured lorries to provide close support. No 2 was an unusual squadron since it is said to have been bought and paid for by the duke himself. This was estimated to have cost over £30,000, which in those days was an immense sum of money. Not that this was entirely necessary; most officers given command of a squadron were not expected to pay for the privilege, but the duke was a special case. Although he was an Army officer (a major in the Cheshire Yeomanry), he was regarded and addressed as a Commander RN whilst in charge of the Armoured Car Squadron. He was also reckoned to be the richest man in Britain, so even £30,000 didn't mean as much to him as it did to other people.

He had served in South Africa during the Boer War, and as he was there when his grandfather died it was then he inherited the title. On the outbreak of the First World War he took his cars – a Rolls-Royce and others – to

LEFT **This is the only picture known to exist of armoured cars in Royal Navy service being shipped to France, probably from Newhaven in Sussex.**

ABOVE No 2 Squadron, Royal Naval Armoured Car Division, under the Duke of Westminster, was sent out to France in March 1915. One of their officers was Anthony Wilding, the New Zealand lawn tennis star. He was tasked with comparing the towed 3pdr gun with the same weapon mounted on a Seabrook armoured lorry. One day when testing a Seabrook, Wilding was killed by a German shell while he rested.

BELOW This is another view of what may be the same car, but it appears to be towing a different gun. It is still a 3pdr, but with a different gun carriage and shield, and running on different wheels.

carried loaded rifles in the car 'just in case' and drove into some very debatable areas.

In November 1914 the duke attached himself to Commander Charles Rumney Samson of the Royal Naval Air Service who, with his band of 'motor bandits' in crude armoured cars, was waging war against the Germans in Flanders. Perhaps this was with a view to the duke taking over his own armoured car squadron in the New Year. Another officer who joined Samson's party was the New Zealand lawn tennis ace Anthony Wilding who served as his transport officer for a while. Wilding had managed to get himself commissioned into the Royal Marines and later went on to serve with No 2 Squadron under the Duke of Westminster. Here he was engaged with assessing the usefulness of the 3-pounder gun which he tested on a wheeled artillery carriage towed by an armoured car and as a self-propelled mounting on a Seabrook lorry. It certainly slowed the armoured car down a bit and affected its manoeuvrability, but being a lot lighter than the Seabrook it was less prone to getting bogged down in the front line and did not present such a large target. Indeed it was on one of these occasions that a lorry got stuck while firing in the direction of the Aubers Ridge and came under German shellfire that Wilding was killed while taking a nap on 9 May 1915.

One of the duke's reasons for having his squadron hurried out to France in March 1915

France as part of what was known as the Royal Automobile Club Corps (although in fact other motoring associations also contributed). This consisted of a number of gentlemen drivers and their cars who acted as chauffeurs for the British High Command. The duke was the regular driver of his friend Major Hugh Dawnay, 2nd Life Guards, who was on the staff of Sir John French. It is said that the duke always

RIGHT This Rolls-Royce is without a machine-gun but it has the initials of the Royal Naval Air Service emblazoned on the side of the bonnet. The meaning of the number '2235' stencilled on the radiator door is unclear; there were never that many armoured cars in service and even Rolls-Royces probably never exceeded 100.

was so that they could participate in the British/Indian attack at Neuve-Chapelle that was launched on 10 March 1915. The battle, fought on a narrow front and plagued by a shortage of artillery ammunition, was a British success at first, but delays and confusion later on caused it ultimately to fail. In any case the British and German trench systems restricted the use of armoured cars and they played no useful part in the battle.

In fact one of the most significant duties

RIGHT A 1914-pattern Rolls-Royce at Southwold in Suffolk during a training run in East Anglia. Note that it is flying the White Ensign, while the officer and man posing on the back are wearing waterproof coats.

BELOW Royal Navy armoured cars outside a hotel at Yelverton in Devon, on the edge of Dartmoor. They may be from No 3 or No 4 Squadrons, prior to being sent out to Gallipoli.

carried out by the armoured cars at this time was what Petty Officer Sam Rolls, one of the drivers, described as taxi duty. This involved picking up staff officers at the White Château on the Poperinghe Road and driving them through Ypres, which was under continual shellfire. With the staff officer sheltering inside the armoured car and a crew member stretched out on a front wing giving directions, the driver sped through Ypres, weaving around the newest shell-holes, and out along the Menin Road to the staff officer's destination.

BELOW **A Rolls-Royce armoured car of No 1 Squadron, Royal Naval Armoured Car Division, is unloaded from a transport on to a raft in Walvis Bay, German South West Africa, before being taken ashore.**

German South West Africa

Although it was not the first to go abroad, No 1 Squadron, Royal Naval Armoured Car Division, was the first to be equipped with turreted Rolls-Royces. Under the command of Lieutenant-Commander W. Whittall, it was sent to Norfolk to work up and to be ready in the event of a German invasion. One thing the men learned during this training period was that the rear springs on the armoured cars were not strong enough. Although the Rolls-Royce chassis had been furnished with extra leaves to the rear springs, bringing the number up to 15 in order to take the weight, it was felt that something stronger was required. Accordingly, all the armoured cars were fitted with much heavier springs at the back to bear the weight.

No 1 Squadron sailed for German South West Africa (now Namibia) in April 1915. They were shipped on an Australian transport, otherwise sailing empty to collect another load, and the plan was to put them ashore in Walfisch (or Walvis) Bay. On arrival they found other shipping ahead of them waiting to unload so, the Navy being an impatient bunch and the ship anxious to get on its way, the men turned to, to unload her. Working without proper cranes, and only the ship's lifting tackle to rely on, the 12 armoured cars, their attendant transport and a mass of stores were lifted over the high sides of the ship and lowered on to rafts to be towed ashore by small tugs.

Since roads were almost unknown outside the settlements and the ground surface was mostly deep sand, Whittall had already decided not to take his heavier vehicles with him. Even the armoured cars weighed about 4 tons apiece and were too heavy for the conditions; it is reasonable to ask what they were doing in the region at all. A few did some good work, but in the most difficult of circumstances. They were acting in support of the ex-Boer commander and South African President General Louis Botha, commanding elements of the South African Army. Besides the obvious value of adding more territory to the British Empire, possession of the coast prevented the establishment of coaling facilities for German surface raiders and denied such vessels a safe place to hide.

By August 1915 the campaign was all over and the Germans defeated, so two-thirds of the squadron was called back to Britain. The other third (four armoured cars) were duly transferred to East Africa, commanded by Alec Nalder, Whittall's second-in-command. They now formed 10 (Royal Navy) Armoured Motor Battery, since the armoured cars had by now been taken over by the War Office although, because Nalder's men insisted that they were still naval personnel, and since there was nobody else out there with their particular skills, they were allowed to remain until they were disbanded in Egypt early in 1917. However, as they were now – to all intents and purposes – an Army unit, their activities will be recorded later.

Gallipoli

In March 1915 No 3 Squadron, commanded by Lieutenant-Commander Josiah Wedgwood MP, left Britain for Gallipoli on the SS *Moorgate.* They were followed the next month by No 4 Squadron (commanded by Lieutenant-Commander James Boothby) on the SS *Inkonka* and in each case one section of four armoured cars was put ashore and installed in special dug-outs on Cape Helles where they were relatively safe from enemy fire. There proved to be little use for armoured cars at Gallipoli, so the other two sections from each squadron remained on their ships; only their machine-guns were dismounted and taken ashore along with their crews, as, for a while, were the weapons and gunners from the eight armoured cars already ashore.

Josiah Wedgwood commanded machine-guns on the collier-cum-assault ship *River Clyde,* while Boothby was in command of some ashore, and it was here that James Boothby was killed on 1 May 1915 at Anzac Cove. Charles Samson was also in the Dardanelles, now in command of No 3 Squadron RNAS, charged with reconnaissance and bombing. Even so, he retained his interest in armoured cars, remarking that in his view they should have gone ashore with the initial landings when they might have been more useful. He also expressed surprise that he was not

ABOVE A Rolls-Royce pictured in a dug-out at Cape Helles on Gallipoli. The officer is thought to be Sub-Lieutenant McLaren.

consulted about them, bearing in mind his earlier experience, particularly by the Army. He seems to have overlooked the fact that the cars themselves were still under Royal Naval command, and indeed one of their commanders, Josiah Wedgwood, had even served with Samson in Flanders.

There is only one recorded occasion when armoured cars went into action on Gallipoli. This was at the Third Battle of Krithia, otherwise known as the Battle of 4 June 1915. Krithia was a village about 2 miles inland from Cape Helles itself and reached by a road of sorts from Sedd el Bahr. It was overlooked by the hill Achi Baba (or Alchi Tepe as it should be known), to which it was the key. Only four of the armoured cars were to be used and the plan was to use them more like tanks (although the tank had not yet been invented at that time). The idea was to have each car fitted with a grapnel device at the end of a long pole sticking out of the back. The cars would reverse up to Krithia, grapple the barbed-wire with their grapnels, and drive away, taking the barbed-wire with them and leaving gaps that the attacking infantry could pass through. An engineer company of the 29th Division smoothed out tracks each side of the Krithia road for the cars to advance along. Moving in line ahead, they set out just after noon on 4 June, described as a brilliant summer's day. Passing through the British lines, each car turned round and began to advance backwards towards Krithia. They were unable to get near enough to the wire to hook into it and therefore proceeded to drive forwards, out of action, all the time under intense rifle and machine-gun fire and some inaccurate shelling. One car had its machine-gun damaged and was ordered to withdraw, another side-slipped off the road and ended up on its side, while a third hit a bump and lost its turret. It is not clear whether any of these things happened before or after they attacked Krithia. In the end all four cars were recovered and, being of no further use, all eight of them left Gallipoli in August for Egypt. They followed the cars that had remained aboard the transports which left for Egypt at the end of June, where they formed the Emergency Squadron based in Alexandria.

BELOW A 1914-pattern turreted Rolls-Royce in mint condition. The location has not been established but note the absence of wooden lockers behind the turret, which suggests this armoured car is in original condition.

In Britain

Two armoured car squadrons remained in Britain; one was No 7 Squadron (twelve Rolls-Royces) and the other was No 14 Squadron comprising six Rolls-Royces, three very similar but underpowered Talbots and three very distinct Delaunay-Bellevilles, probably assembled in France. Of the nine other cars that were not issued to squadrons, one had its turret removed and replaced by a Vickers 1-pounder

Pom-Pom, a type of heavy machine-gun on a pedestal mount (probably the naval Mark 2 version) with a calibre of 1.457 inches (near enough 37mm) and a range of around 4,000yd firing a high-explosive shell. Conceived as a mobile close support for the ordinary armoured cars, the drawback with this vehicle was that the gunner could only fire the weapon, which had 360-degree traverse, by clambering all over the vehicle – anywhere but within the fighting compartment – since there appears to have been no room. Ultimately this project seems to have been abandoned and the car refitted with its turret. It is the only known modification of a Rolls-Royce in naval service.

On 16 February 1915, Commodore Murray Sueter, Director of the Admiralty Air Department, organised a display on Horse Guards Parade which Winston Churchill, First Lord of the Admiralty was to attend. The key exhibit in the display was a horse-drawn truck fitted with the Pedrail patent track system which Sueter wanted the First Lord to see. Sueter also arranged to take along a Rolls-Royce armoured car because he wanted the two ideas to be associated in the First Lord's head. The idea

was that an armoured car, fitted with tracks, would be a good solution to the trench problem that was playing on the First Lord's mind. From his subsequent writings there is no actual evidence that Churchill drew that impression at all. He pushed the tracked truck around and noted how easy it was to move, but that seems to be as far as his understanding went.

A demonstration of progress in armoured vehicle development was held at Barlby Road on 30 June 1915. It was attended by, among others, David Lloyd George, the newly appointed Minister of Munitions, and Winston Churchill, former First Lord of the Admiralty. Among the exhibits was a Rolls-Royce armoured car, maybe even the same one that had been seen on Horse Guards Parade in February. The armoured car was towing a 3-pounder gun, a 47mm weapon on a two-wheeled carriage. Such guns were already in use in France, by Samson and Wilding among others, but the version shown at Barlby Road was a much more substantial affair with a large shield, a hefty steel trail and narrow steel wheels, albeit in pairs on each side, with solid rubber tyres. It actually looks too heavy – even for a Rolls-Royce – to pull across broken ground such as you might find on the Western Front.

In Russia

Finally we should mention the one, or maybe two Rolls-Royce armoured cars that served with Oliver Locker-Lampson's Russian Armoured Car Division that was formed in Britain in October 1915, but did all its fighting to begin with on the Eastern Front. It only appears to have had one Rolls-Royce armoured car (although some sources say two); most of its armoured cars were Lanchesters from Nos 5, 6 and 15 Squadrons, minus three on loan to the Belgian Army. During a return visit to London in October 1915, Locker-Lampson attempted to trade his Lanchesters for Rolls-Royces, but this did not prove possible. By his arrogant flouting of their authority, he had already made enemies of some of the Board of Admiralty, but in any case by now these cars had all been transferred to the War Office and were no longer available. The one known Rolls-Royce with the unit appears to have been commanded by Lieutenant-Commander Wells Hood. The Rolls-Royce is first mentioned during the fighting in Rumania in December 1916, when it and two Lanchesters attacked the Bulgarian trenches in dreadful conditions. Both Lanchesters became bogged down in the mud and despite tightening up their epicyclic

ABOVE **The Royal Naval Armoured Car Division at Barlby Road also built a 3pdr gun on a wheeled carriage to be towed by a Rolls-Royce armoured car. It was a much more professional product than those cobbled together in France, but far too heavy to be towed except as here, on the sports ground behind the Clement Talbot Works.**

the crew preferring to ride outside. There were other armoured car actions, but the Rolls-Royce is never mentioned again. It may have survived, but with the Russian Revolution imminent and the men preparing to depart, whatever remaining armoured cars there were had to be left behind. However, it is worth remarking that at a reunion dinner in May 1919 Locker-Lampson was presented with a silver model of an armoured car and it was a Rolls-Royce, not a Lanchester.

Egypt

It seems that armoured cars were used in operations in the Egyptian desert even before the Duke of Westminster and his force arrived. These cars must have come from the Emergency Squadron which was formed in Alexandria in September 1915 and joined the Western Frontier Force in November, although this is not actually stated anywhere. Even so, they were only used sparingly, without the dash normally exhibited by a good commander.

The Emergency Squadron was comprised of those cars, Rolls-Royces of course, of Nos 3 and 4 Squadrons that did not go ashore at Gallipoli. The figure usually given is 12 cars, but if all squadrons were complete and only 4 cars from each squadron went ashore, then it should really have been 16. Cars from the Emergency Squadron served with the Western Frontier Force from November 1915 until April 1916, by which time the 8 cars from Gallipoli should also have been available. There is a photograph

ABOVE This is the Rolls-Royce armoured car that accompanied Locker-Lampson's force to Russia. It is seen in Galicia, with a Lanchester behind it.

BELOW The Emergency Squadron in Alexandria, which was the balance of Nos 3 and 4 Squadrons that were not landed on Gallipoli.

gears could not be extricated. The Rolls-Royce went into action alone and then came out. The remainder of the Lanchester crews, with the exception of Lieutenant Ingles, who was given up for dead, were taken away as prisoners. Ingles managed to crawl back to the Russian lines and the abandoned cars appear to have been recovered later, by the Rolls-Royce according to one source. In June the following year it was in action again, with other vehicles, against the Germans in Austrian Galicia, and although successful at first, the attack failed when the Russian infantry lost heart.

A little further south, at Kamiloovka, the vehicle saw further action in July but during the retreat was set on fire by artillery and was driven out of action with great difficulty, most of

of 20 Rolls-Royce armoured cars, taken at Mustapha Barracks, in the booklet *Rolls-Royce Armoured Cars and the Great Victory*.

Actions in the Western Desert were directed against the Senussi. The Senussi was a Sufi Muslim sect, or brotherhood, founded in the early 19th century to improve religious observances among the peoples of the desert. They appear to have been no threat to anybody, although for some reason they did not like the Italians or the French. However, they got on well with the Egyptians and the people of Palestine and with the British and Turks. German money and Turkish blandishments turned them into a warlike force, but the reason why the British declared war on them was connected with the loss of the armed steamer HMS *Tara* and the transport ship SS *Moorina*. Both were torpedoed by a German submarine and their crews brought ashore and handed into the care of the Senussi. Attempts by the British to negotiate their release were rejected by the Senussi, who were under the influence of Turkish advisers. For this reason the British declared war on them as they were seen as allies of the Central Powers.

On 27 January 1916 the Royal Naval Armoured Car Division was duly replaced by the Cavalry Corps Motor Machine-Gun Battery, according to the Official History, comprising 17 armoured cars and 21 motorcycles, presumably the renamed Emergency Squadron since there was no other known source of armoured cars.

Under War Office command

In *Steel Chariots in the Desert* Sam Rolls says that, while they were still in France, their commanding officer, the Duke of Westminster, advised them to transfer from the Navy to the Army if they wanted to remain with the armoured cars. Although the official date of the change to War Office control is given as August 1915, it seems to have been a gradual process, taking the rest of the year, while in one case – Oliver Locker-Lampson's Russian Armoured Car Division – it never happened at all.

The Duke of Westminster, having arrived in Egypt, now wearing the uniform of a major in the Cheshire Yeomanry, took his squadron of 12 Rolls-Royces along the coast to Mersa Matruh by sea. To conform with military requirements, his unit was now divided into three Armoured Motor Batteries, each of four cars and numbered 1st, 2nd and 3rd. So although his original naval squadron had been subdivided into three sections, it still functioned under the duke as an Armoured Car Brigade of 12 Rolls-Royces – in effect nothing had changed, although the sections had now become independent batteries. There was a road of sorts, running west through the desert from Alexandria, known as the Khedivial Motor Road. It kept close to the coast and even passed through Matruh, but the desert was in such a state of tumult – with the Senussites moving around in unknown numbers and parties of Egyptian Bedouin Arabs ready to attack anyone

BELOW Two armoured cars that served with 8th (Cyclist's Battalion) the Essex Regiment – a fate that awaited a number of vehicles when the War Office took over.

ABOVE **Working on a Silver Ghost chassis, although there is no guarantee in this case that it is from an armoured car.**

if they thought they could win – that it was deemed safer to move the armoured cars by sea. The duke's original squadron included three Seabrook armoured lorries, which were classed as heavy armoured cars. These had accompanied the force to the desert but the duke felt that they were too heavy to operate over sand and in any case too slow to keep pace with the armoured cars, therefore they were limited to operating along the coastal road. Meanwhile, what were considered the light armoured cars, weighing approximately 4 tons each, operated alone.

Early in the morning of 17 March 1916, the duke, with 45 vehicles including armoured cars, light patrol cars and ambulances, set out on the mission that was to hit the headlines everywhere and bring him and his armoured cars fame. The mission was the rescue of the surviving crews of HMS *Tara* and SS *Moorina*. They had been located at El Hakkim, 120 miles from Sollum, and it was 3.00pm when the duke's column arrived. All told, 91 men were rescued and although the event is heavily dramatised by Sam Rolls, it was clearly a tense affair, which included the massacre of most of the jailers and their families. According to Sam Rolls, once the captives had been freed and

LEFT **A Rolls-Royce armoured car said to have belonged to the Duke of Westminster's force in the Western Desert.**

while they were receiving emergency treatment, the duke set off in a fast car to report the success of the operation. This would probably have been the duke's own Rolls-Royce Silver Ghost tourer, which he had taken with him and invariably drove around in the desert with a Maxim machine-gun on a tripod in the back.

ABOVE Undertaking fairly major repairs in the open desert was not recommended, but sometimes it just had to be done. Notice how the headlamps on the right-hand car have been reversed, perhaps to save the glass.

Ireland

Six Rolls-Royce armoured cars were shipped across to Dublin in 1916, probably in response to events provoked by the Easter Rising. They were among the first armoured vehicles used in Ireland and it was probably one of the first times that the War Office had deployed armoured vehicles since they were taken over from the Royal Navy.

Since this was before the establishment of the Machine Gun Corps (Motors), the Army did not, as yet, have a trained corps of armoured car crews, never mind drivers, so these appear to have been recruited from infantry units already out there, perhaps with drivers drawn from the Army Service Corps. The only picture

BELOW Dublin, 1916: a Rolls-Royce alongside an armoured Crossley tender with a wire roof to shield passengers from missiles.

we have seen of one of these cars so far shows it on a city street in company with another military vehicle, possibly a tender, carrying infantry. The two perhaps acted as a fast-reaction unit sent to tackle a local trouble spot.

East Africa

The campaign in East Africa, mainly and latterly in German East Africa, lasted from 1914 until the end of 1918. It was fought on the Allied side by British, Indian and South African troops along with Belgian and in places Portuguese troops. Much of the country fought over was unreconstructed bush where roads were few and appalling, the climate unforgiving, against an enemy under the command of a brilliant and elusive soldier Colonel von Lettow-Vorbeck. Originally, command of Allied Forces was to be given to General Sir Horace Smith-Dorrien, the man credited with saving the BEF in 1914 when he was a brigade commander but which got him into trouble with the Commander-in-Chief Sir John French, leading to his dismissal from that position. Smith-Dorrien felt that the key to containing the Germans in East Africa was mobility, so he requested a strong force of armoured cars. As a result, three Rolls-Royce units were earmarked: 10th (Royal Navy) Armoured Motor Battery (10 (RN) AMB), part of the force which had done so well in German South West Africa, which served there throughout 1916 and saw what action there was, and 4th and 5th Light Armoured

Batteries, each with four armoured cars, formed in Britain and sent out in February 1916. Each battery was attached to a different force but saw no real action. Later they were joined by 1 (Willoughby's) Armoured Motor Battery, also known as 322 Company Army Service Corps, equipped with four Leyland armoured lorries which proved to be too heavy for conditions out there and saw little service: 'they only rarely encountered the enemy and had little influence on the campaign', according to one writer.[1] Even the Rolls-Royces found the conditions difficult and were often limited to patrolling in conjunction with the mounted infantry.

Horace Smith-Dorrien caught pneumonia and had to be invalided home and his replacement as C-in-C was the South African Jan Christian Smuts, now a general, who took over in February 1916 and established under himself a largely South African-led army. Smuts also made a case for invading German East Africa, rather against the wishes of Lord Kitchener as expressed in his Instructions to General Sir H. Smith-Dorrien which he issued on 18 December 1915.

In a sense this had already been compromised by the disastrous landings at Tanga in November 1914, but since then most of the action seems to have been focused on the Uganda Railway, which the Germans raided on a regular basis. Armoured cars were deemed to be one of the best methods of

---

1   B.T. White, *Tanks and Other Armoured Fighting Vehicles 1900 to 1918*, Blandford Press, 1970.

BELOW A newspaper image showing the Royal Navy detachment sent to East Africa.

controlling this, working in conjunction with the Mounted Infantry and in due course they had the threat to the railway under control, the Germans starting to find such raids unprofitable.

The action against German positions on and around Salaita Hill in February 1916 appears to be the only occasion in the campaign when armoured cars made any real contribution to the fighting. Two of the four armoured cars of 10 (RN) AMB managed to break through some thick, almost impenetrable bush, which brought them out in rear of some German trenches which they swept with machine-gun fire. However, they were fired on in return and for a while it looked as though they were trapped, since they could not find the path that they had come in by. Ultimately it was found by an escorting motorcyclist and they were able to withdraw. In no way could the action be described as a success; although massively outnumbering the Germans, the Allied Forces were defeated and had to retreat. The Germans were employing an old Boer trick – occupying hidden trenches at the foot of the hill while leaving those on the crest unoccupied. Again this revealed the mastery of the German commander Colonel von Lettow-Vorbeck, although even he could not be right all the time, even saying in an account written after the war:

> The troops at New Steglitz advanced to Taveta, where some fantastic reports came in about hostile armoured cars, which were alleged to be moving through the thorn bush desert. The imagination of the natives, to whom these armoured cars were something altogether new and surprising, had made them see ghosts.

To the African troops on both sides the armoured cars were *kifaru* (rhinos), and it was said that if they had not been present the final stages of the battle would have been a massacre. There is a reference, in the volume of the Official History covering the campaign in East Africa, which says the four naval cars of

RIGHT Rolls-Royces in East Africa. Again, a spare wheel is missing from the nearest car, otherwise they appear to be in original condition.

ABOVE This Rolls-Royce in Army service in East Africa has an extension added to the turret roof, a shield covering the machine-gun aperture, but no spare wheel on the left side.

the 4th Light Armoured Car Battery (4th LACB), commanded by Lieutenant-Commander W. Whittall, left Mbuyuni on 7 April 1916, crossed the Sanya river but once the annual rains started became bogged down every few miles and did not reach Arusa until four weeks later. By this time nearly half the personnel were stricken with disease or dysentery and did not make it as far as the front at Kondoa Irangi until the last week in May. The only trouble with this account is that elsewhere 4th LACB is understood to be a Machine Gun Corps formation and the only formation out there with any Royal Navy connection is said to be 10th Armoured Motor Battery.

Lieutenant-Commander Whittall, who had commanded No 1 Squadron RNAS in German South West Africa (of which 10th AMB was an offshoot), certainly returned to East Africa but now as a major. It seems he commanded 4th LACB after Captain Goldberg, the brigade's original commander. In a later footnote it is said that one armoured car broke down at Lolkisale, a second at Ufiome and a third when they arrived at Kondoa Irangi, whereupon, three days after their arrival, the machine-guns were removed and employed in the line. However, the breakdowns are unlikely to have been permanent, because two armoured cars of 4th Light Armoured Battery are said, in the text, to have been made ready to participate in General van Deventer's further advance early in June 1916, presumably with their machine-guns restored. By this time the seasonal rains were over and the roads, such as they were, were rapidly drying out. Miles Thomas, later a senior executive in the Nuffield group, was serving as a private, a Rolls-Royce armoured car driver with 4th Light Armoured Battery. He recounts the wet weather that turned the tracks to mud and brought the armoured cars to a halt, plus the serious outbreak of disease that decimated the crews. He also tells a story of using a herd of cattle, driven ahead of the armoured cars, which acted as mine detectors by setting off improvised land mines on the road as they went over them.

By July 1918 three armoured cars of 4th Light Armoured Battery were sent to join the Mounted Brigade at Itiso-kwa-Meda, but they were sent back to Haneti to join the infantry when it was discovered that beyond Itiso the terrain was totally unsuitable for such vehicles. Even so, the armoured cars were proving valuable, despite enemy land mines and booby traps along the roads, and the crews were congratulated on their work. They seem to have survived unscathed in the cars, although the heat inside the armour was very unpleasant. The only reported trouble was with the unarmoured petrol tanks, which were badly holed.

But according to Miles Thomas, he was one of four drivers sent with their Rolls-Royces by sea to Egypt via Dar-es-Salaam in April 1917, whereupon 4th Light Armoured Battery was apparently disbanded.

Salonika

Two Rolls-Royce armoured cars were sent to Salonika in January 1916; they belonged to 6th Armoured Motor Battery but they were sent without crews and it is not clear whether crews were provided from the infantry already there or if the cars were simply stored. Later, crews were found, but there is no record of them doing anything significant beyond perhaps a bit of local patrolling. They are mentioned once in the Official History of the war in Macedonia (vol. 1) when they arrive. They are mentioned again in vol. 2 when they depart, but nothing in between suggests that they were not called upon to do very much.

They were in Egypt by May 1917, where two further armoured cars were acquired, although it was understood when they left Macedonia that they were required for Mesopotamia. They did not go there until August 1917 when, expanded to become 6th LAMB, we encounter them again.

On the Western Front

Meanwhile, three Light Armoured Batteries – 7th, 8th and 9th – were sent to the Western Front in March 1916. We don't know a lot about them except that one armoured car was photographed at Guillemont on the Somme escorting an ambulance and another is seen, well behind the lines, at Abbeville. Their opportunity for action does not come until the eve of the Battle of Arras. One battery of

RIGHT Armoured cars on the Western Front were quite rare. This Rolls-Royce was photographed escorting an ambulance at Guillemont, on the Somme in September 1916. The turret, which is surmounted by a protected lookout, is reversed. The car has no front mudguards, but there appears to be the remains of a device fitted at the front to drag away barbed wire.

four Rolls-Royces, commanded by a Captain Ronan, were used against the village of Roisel on 26 March 1917 in conjunction with the 18th Bengal Lancers. Two cars swept around the outside to chase off the German cavalry while the other pair entered the village and engaged the garrison who were forced to withdraw. The Germans arranged for an instant counter-attack but the armoured cars held them off until sufficient infantry arrived to hold the captured village. The following day the same four cars were used against the village of Villers-Faucon,

RIGHT The Battle of Arras in April 1917 was one of the few occasions when tanks and armoured cars took part in the same action, although there is no evidence that they ever met. The two cars shown here carry fancy camouflage schemes and have a raised section on top of their turrets. They are also clad in a mineral substance called 'Uralite', which was supposed to diminish the effect of armour-piercing bullets.

LEFT One of the camouflaged Rolls-Royces in Arras was seen towing a 47mm (3pdr) gun on an improvised carriage. Note that although the machine-gun mounts an extra shield, there is no elevated top to the turret and no front mudguards, but the car is fitted with a barbed wire-removing device.

ABOVE This armoured car stuck in the mud at Arras clearly shows the wire-clearing device and the rod that activates it. Notice, too, the raised look-out on the turret roof and the cladding of Uralite.

BELOW Two Uralite-clad Rolls-Royces in an Arras street. Notice that chains have been fitted to the back wheels on account of the mud.

along with some cavalry of the 8th Hussars, but the Germans here were equipped with machine-guns firing armour-piercing bullets, and when two cars heading towards the village became trapped in a large crater, three men were killed. In the end the cavalry came in on the flank and the village was captured, so it appeared for a while that a combination of cavalry and armoured cars was the ideal combination for such work. Some armoured cars, probably belonging to 8th Light Armoured

Battery (since one was towing a 3-pounder gun), were photographed at Tilloy-les-Mofflaines on the edge of Arras in April 1917. The cars were camouflage-painted and covered in a mineral substance called Uralite, which was intended to enhance the level of protection. It is not known what these armoured cars did, if anything, but since tanks were also deployed during the Battle of Arras, they were at least operating in the same area and might just have been in contact.

There is no evidence of armoured cars being used during the Third Battle of Ypres, but conditions were so bad that even tanks had great difficulty, and by October 1917 they had all gone, mostly to the Middle East. There were therefore none available to take part in the Battle of Cambrai (20 November 1917) where they might have been more useful.

Western Desert and Palestine

Back in the Middle East the focus had now moved from the Western Desert to the defence of the Suez Canal and from there into northern Egypt and up towards Palestine. The Egyptian Expeditionary Force, at first under the command of General Sir Archibald Murray and later of Sir Edmund Allenby, numbered in its ranks Nos 11 and 12 Light Armoured Car Batteries, which had been made up from cars taken out of the Royal Navy's Emergency Squadron. They were subsequently joined by Nos 2 and 3 Armoured Motor Batteries, also with four cars each. There is some evidence to suggest that men from the Australian Armoured Car Section patrolled in borrowed Rolls-Royces when their own vehicles proved to be unsuitable for desert conditions and before they were converted to the 1st (Australian) Light Car Patrol and equipped with Model T Fords. Indeed, it seems likely that it was the Australians who favoured operating the Rolls-Royces with the upper panels of their turrets removed (and the top panels of the bonnet as well); however, we are not able to verify this, either here or in Australia.

The cars in British service are listed as 'Machine Gun Corps', and thus are classified with the artillery, but most of their work was

LEFT In a scene that illustrates the difficulties of desert travel, this car with an Australian crew member appears to be sinking in the sand and the running boards have been removed. In order to reduce the effects of heat the top panels from the turret are gone as are those covering the engine.

RIGHT A classic view of a Rolls-Royce in the Western Desert. The top panels of the turret have been removed to help reduce the heat inside, but four Antipodeans have crowded in to have their photograph taken. The hinged plates over the engine have also been removed to aid cooling and another Australian is lounging at the front.

done with the cavalry. After seeing some action in the Western Desert, they went north and were attached to the mounted troops, the Australian Light Horse and the New Zealand Mounted Rifles. They served during the three Battles of Gaza; during the First Battle of Gaza they are mentioned as working with the 3rd Light Horse to hold off a Turkish attack out of Huj. During the Third Battle of Gaza in November 1917, 11th LACB, with 1st (Australian) Light Car Patrol were sent along the Hebron Road, north-east from Beersheba, with instructions to occupy the village of Dhariya but to recce tracks and look for sources of water on the way. A few days later, on 7 November 1917, 11th and 12th LACB, working with the Desert Mounted Corps, had to be left on the Hebron Road while the cavalry, with 1st

RIGHT Even Rolls-Royces got captured now and then. This one is in German hands in Palestine, apparently in good condition, although the turret has been reversed.

LEFT Photographed in Jerusalem soon after the war, this Rolls-Royce carries extra spare wheels but no headlamps.

(Australian) Light Car Patrol moved into the mountains where Rolls-Royce armoured cars were deemed to be too heavy to go owing to the underdeveloped terrain. This illustrates one of the points held against the use of vehicles in that hilly country when compared with traditional cavalry. On 14 November 1917 two armoured cars from 12th LACB, then waiting at Mesmiye, were told to attack Junction Station, then heavily defended by the Turks. Junction Station is on the line west of Jerusalem and the

ABOVE Two Rolls-Royces pictured in Alexandria. That on the left is missing its front mudguard. The style of dress seems to suggest a post-war picture, but the cars appear unmodified.

RIGHT From an old postcard, another Rolls-Royce seen in Alexandria, probably shortly after the war.

two cars advanced down the road, firing their machine-guns and driving the enemy out before handing the place over to the 123rd Rifles. On 20 November 1917 two cars from 12th LACB were used to provide covering fire for the 2nd/4th Somerset Light Infantry for an attack against the village of Salis. On 24 November 1917 3rd Armoured Motor Battery supported an attack by the Wellington Regiment (New Zealand cavalry) against Hadra Bridge on the Nahr el Auja river. Four days later one armoured car from 2nd AMB was employed to oppose a flanking movement by the Turks against the yeomanry on high ground at Hellabi during a counter-attack. Many of these were small, insignificant actions, although they are a foretaste of things to come as armoured cars proved their worth and become more acceptable to Allenby's Army.

On 27 December 1917 two cars from 3rd AMB were included in the defence of Jerusalem which, having been captured, was now under fierce attack by Turkish forces. During the fighting one of the armoured cars reversed off the road and became bogged down; it was abandoned and came under fire from Turkish artillery.

While fighting in the Jordan Valley on 1 May 1918, only two cars from 12th LACB were available; the other two had developed mechanical trouble and been sent to Ghoraniye for overnight repairs. Of the two surviving cars one reversed into a deep rut and had to be abandoned, while the other had to fight until it suffered too many casualties and ran short of ammunition.

As time wore on and confidence grew, more use was made of armoured cars in their own right. Particularly in the confused fighting north-west of Jerusalem, at Haifa, Acre, Damascus and Aleppo.

At the Battle of Megiddo on 21 September 1918, cars from 2nd AMB advanced up the Nablus Road from Tul Karm. Two armoured cars were in the force that took Nablus.

The next day, 22 September 1918, 12th LACB with 7th Light Car Patrol (LCP) was sent towards Haifa with a view to capturing it. Unfortunately they ran into a roadblock before they got there, came under fire from machine-guns and artillery and had to extricate themselves.

On 23 September 1918 11th LACB advanced towards Acre and found the place undefended.

ABOVE A Rolls-Royce in service with 11 Light Armoured Motor Battery (LAMB), which has a shield fitted over the machine-gun aperture, but no headlamps. The dog sitting on the open body top looks too large for a mascot and is probably somebody's pet.

On 25 September 12th LACB, now at Nazareth, advanced towards Tiberias which it duly entered and captured.

Meanwhile, on 29 September 1918, 11th LACB was sent along the Damascus Road

BELOW Another car serving with 11 LAMB. This one also has a shield over the machine-gun aperture and a profusion of spare tyres, but it looks a bit battered, especially the front mudguards. Note, also, that it has no markings.

ABOVE An armoured car and two Model T Fords, the opposite ends of the social scale in motoring terms, but both ideal for desert operations. Once again at least one Australian and the inevitable dog are in the picture; note, too, the quantity of luggage on the running board and the generous mass of extra spare tyres.

when it ran into a defensive position at Sa' Sa' which it could not overcome. In fact it was not defeated until the following morning, when reinforcements arrived.

On 6 October 1918, 14th Cavalry Brigade, supported by 12th LACB and 7th LCP, were ordered north from Damascus to Riyaq where it was reported that much damage was being done to the railway installation. What had been originally planned as an urgent overnight trip was held back until the next day. Although much damage was discovered, fortunately most of the railway equipment was still intact.

Then, on 18 October 1918, three armoured car units – 2nd AMB, 11th and 12th LACB – with 1st (Australian), 2nd and 8th Light Car Patrols with 5th Cavalry Brigade were despatched from Homs towards Aleppo.

One action, on 22 October 1918, involved three armoured car units – 2nd, 11th and 12th – and the (Australian) Light Car Patrol with six Model T Fords, each armed with a Lewis gun. The armoured cars were called out to pursue a Turkish rearguard travelling in lorries escorted by a large German armoured car on the road to Aleppo. The British armoured cars, all Rolls-Royces, chased the German car, firing as they

LEFT At the end of the First World War a few cars, mainly from Glasgow, appeared with taller turrets on 1914-style bodies. Not much is known about them, but this one has the later style of British registration plate.

went along, and forced it to surrender, while the Australians captured one of the lorries (although in the British Official History the lorry is said to have broken down and the passengers scattered). It may well be the only action involving British armoured cars and a German vehicle of the same type to be recorded from the First World War.

Aleppo was captured on 25 September 1918 and on the next day 12th LACB was sent north-west to attack Haritan where it came under intense rifle fire and had to withdraw for the time being. The Turkish position was overcome that night and it turned out to be the last action against the Turks in the First World War; they capitulated a few days later.

With Lawrence in Arabia

What began as the Hedjaz Section apparently consisted of two armoured cars that had originally served with 10th (Royal Naval) Armoured Motor Battery in East Africa and later two armed tenders named *Blast* and *Bloodhound* that had originally been armoured cars serving with the Duke of Westminster's force in the Egyptian desert. Both were converted to tenders in Alexandria.

According to one source they were first landed at Wejh, halfway down the Red Sea coast, where the terrain proved unsuitable and so were then shipped up the Gulf of Aqaba to be landed at Aqaba, which troops of the Arab Revolt had captured from the Turks. They were joined by two armed tenders from 1st Armoured Motor Battery in December 1917 which became a battery again when the other two cars joined in June 1918. This force was disbanded at Suez in October 1918 when Turkey surrendered.

T.E. Lawrence described going into action in a Rolls-Royce armoured car as 'Fighting de-luxe' and wrote that 'a Rolls in the desert is above rubies'; however, he furnishes no consecutive account of their actions. He certainly used an armoured car during an attack on the Amman Bridge of the Hedjaz Railway in September 1918. Lawrence also refers to a Rolls-Royce tender named *Blue Mist* which apparently gave excellent service but, since the armoured cars were under British

command and manned by British crews, it seems reasonable to suppose that at times they operated independently of Lawrence with other elements of Prince Faisal's army.

The Hedjaz Armoured Car Section War Diary begins on 1 April 1918 when they are based at Gueira. At first it is a sequence of parades and training but Lieutenant Colonel Lawrence turns up in a Ford car on the afternoon of 13 April, so clearly something is imminent. A raid was being planned to wreck the railway at Tel-el-Shamin to prevent reinforcements arriving at Maan – the main focus of an Arab attack. The attacking force consisted of three Rolls-Royce armoured cars, two 10-pounder field guns in tenders, two Rolls-Royce tenders and three Ford vans. They were supported by elements of the Royal Flying Corps, a 75mm gun of the Egyptian Camel Corps and about 200 Arabs on camels. Lieutenant Colonels Lawrence and Dawnay observed from a nearby hill. A series of attacks was organised on Turkish posts in the area, a number of culverts were destroyed and ultimately Tel-el-Shamin station was attacked. The garrison surrendered but there were no Allied casualties. On 20 April one armoured car, accompanied by Lawrence, Dawnay and Captain Hornby RE, was sent to investigate Ramleh station but found that it had been evacuated to Medowara station 10 miles further south so the buildings were destroyed and a section of track blown up. Reconnaissance showed that Medowara station was too strongly held to attack so the force moved against Wadi Rethem station, the next one north. The station was again found to be abandoned but it was covered by a position on a nearby hill which included artillery that outranged the British guns. Meanwhile, one armoured car had become ditched and had to be temporarily abandoned. The ground around Wadi Rethem station was found to be rough and stony but the station buildings were blown up along with a ten-arch culvert a bit further south and another section of track.

In May further raids were organised against the railway, mostly to blow up bridges. The section was reinforced by the arrival of two more armoured cars and a Wolseley tender, and with these vehicles another raid was organised against Jerdun station and bridges in

ABOVE T.E. Lawrence (of Arabia) enters Damascus in a Rolls-Royce tender (once an armoured car) named *Blast* driven by S.C. (Sam) Rolls.

BELOW Rolls-Royces of the Hedjaz Squadron that served with Lawrence of Arabia. They are fitted with double front wheels for operating over soft sand.

the vicinity. Arab infantry were sent forward to capture the station, supported by two armoured cars, but the building was again found to be abandoned. Some bridges and a length of track were blown up, whereupon it was learned that a 300-strong Turkish force was advancing against the Arabs. While these men were withdrawn, two armoured cars moved up to confront the Turks. Fire from the cars proved decisive and the enemy broke and fled.

Major Maynard, who had led this expedition, then organised a raid by the detachment against a 12-arch bridge at Bir-el-Shadie. This was duly destroyed and the force returned to camp. June was mostly taken up with reconnaissances, including one to Jedrun station, which was found to have been reoccupied and entrenched. The cars began to

fire upon the trenches until a Turkish armoured train turned up and they had to withdraw out of range. During one run a front wheel on a Model T Ford collapsed and the vehicle turned over. It had to be abandoned but was later recovered and repaired.

Once again, in July reconnaissances were the order of the day, including one to Jedrun station. Here they hoped to provoke an attack, but nothing happened so they withdrew. However, while in the area they came across a five-man Turkish cavalry patrol, all of whom were duly captured. In August, in addition to numerous reconnaissances, an attempt was made to cross the railway near Jedrun at dusk, but the Turks had established a strong defensive position and an attack by Sherifian infantry was called off. The armoured cars, as the main targets, were heavily peppered and some damage was sustained; but as no casualties were reported they withdrew.

By September the enemy were clearly withdrawing but one large attack was mounted, which Colonel Lawrence attended, at Umptaive, in company with Sherifian forces. Although they were both damaged and their tyres shredded, the armoured cars played a dominant part, even taking on the armoured train when it turned up. In the end they drove in a strong enemy force, attempting to repair a damaged bridge and blew up even more of it.

By early November 1918 what remained of the force was located in Damascus and the

fighting was over. On 1 January 1919 they were told that the Hedjaz Armoured Car Section no longer existed and that it was now No 1 Battery, Light Armoured Cars, but demobilisation was imminent and the force was dwindling. The final diary entry is dated 21 January 1919.

Mesopotamia

Although two armoured cars were present at the Battle of Ctesiphon in November 1915, we have no idea what make they were, or where they came from. The first mention of Rolls-Royce armoured cars is from an account of a projected attack on Ramadi, on the Euphrates south of Baghdad on 11 July 1917. Four cars from 14th Light Armoured Motor Battery were sent forward on reconnaissance but were stopped at the Euphrates Valley Canal, a new cut which linked the river with Lake Habbaniya. The canal proved too wide and too deep to be crossed by armoured cars, so they returned to Lieutenant Colonel Haldane with useful information regarding Turkish dispositions on the other side. Later they were sent back to the canal to engage Turkish positions on the left while a sapper detachment was sent to build a crossing point for the cars, but it is not clear whether they were able to complete this. In any case, due to the heat and dust storms, the attack was called off.

Meanwhile, in September 1917 6th and 15th LAMBs arrived in Mesopotamia from Egypt. 15th LAMB seems to have had its full complement of eight Rolls-Royces, although 6th LAMB only had four. These were two that were brought along from Salonika (as 6th AMB) plus two more picked up in Egypt. Its other four armoured cars were Leylands (ex-Willoughby's No 1 AMB from East Africa), but it disposed of these soon after it arrived in Mesopotamia.

On 24 September 1917 four armoured cars from 14th LAMB, working with 7th Cavalry Brigade, mounted an attack on Mandali which was successful and which they occupied by the morning of the 28th.

The attack on Ramadi was renewed on 28 September 1917, this time involving four armoured cars from 13th LAMB and 6th Cavalry Brigade. They crossed the Euphrates Canal

(otherwise the Habbaniya Escape or Habbaniya Canal) but were held up by the Aziziya Canal which, although dry had very steep sides and was too soft at the bottom for horses, never mind armoured cars. Ramps and a bridge were built, which took until 12.30pm, and after resting 6th Cavalry Brigade pushed on to get behind the Turkish defenders while the armoured cars covered the flank. The main attack was now in the hands of 12th and 42nd Brigades, while the cavalry's role was to stop the Turks from retreating and so capture them. As the main action ended, the armoured cars were sent about 10 miles along the road to Hit, looking for any Turks who might have escaped; they found none. An attempt was made to raid Hit on 2 October 1917, using the armoured cars and 1st/4th Dorsets carried in Fords, but they arrived too late and surprise was lost. Even so, the armoured cars exchanged fire with Hit garrison before the whole raiding force withdrew.

The Jabal Hamrin is a narrow, rugged range of hills running in a north-westerly direction, some distance north of Baghdad. It was the focus of attention on 20 October 1917. General Maude's intention was to drive the Turks out of the hills but this required operations on both sides. Two armoured cars from 6th LAMB, in combination with two from 14th LAMB, were sent to work with 7th Cavalry Brigade while two more cars from 6th LAMB worked with 12th Cavalry. The latter appear to have done nothing of note, although those with 7th Cavalry Brigade, after the main force had occupied Qizil Ribat on the other side of the hills, was sent about 6 miles along the road to Khaniqin looking for retreating Turks. Again they found none.

Four days later, on 24 October 1917, the same cars were used to attack Turkish positions at Huwaislat but discovered the trenches empty and the position abandoned.

The next action involving armoured cars was the attack on Daur which began on 2 November 1917. It involved cars from 13th, 14th and 15th LAMB, attached to the Cavalry Division and two cars from 6th LAMB working with 21st Brigade on the other side of the Tigris. The attack on Daur was ultimately successful, so on 5 November the force moved north along the river to assault Tikrit. Tikrit itself was strongly held with a maze of trenches all around

ABOVE This photograph was taken outside the American College at Aintab in Kurdistan, sometime in 1919. Notice that no front brakes are fitted; Rolls-Royce did not introduce front brakes on their cars until 1924. Again, three Australians appear to have turned up along with a young man who is unlikely to be one of the crew.

it, but repeated attacks by infantry and cavalry caused the Turks to abandon their trenches and withdraw to the north. Once again the armoured cars of 6th LAMB with 21st Brigade were operating east of the river but in neither action does the Official History record any activities specific to the armoured cars.

Lieutenant-Colonel C.L. Matthews was in command of Matthews' Column, which included two armoured cars from 6th LAMB, some cavalry, artillery, a machine-gun company and Matthews' own regiment, the 1st/4th Hampshires. Although ostensibly a detached part of General Marshall's command, Matthews' Column was moving into an area of western Persia which was dominated by Dunsterforce under Major-General Lionel Dunsterville. They were heading for Baku on the Caspian Sea in what in those days was Russian Azerbaijan. Post-Revolutionary Russia was in an incredible state of flux. Baku itself was in the hands of the Bolsheviks, although under attack by the Turks, while a loyalist Russian detachment under Colonel Bicharakov was in Persia and anxious to co-operate with British forces.

In April 1918 Dunsterville was at Hamadan, west of Teheran, where he was joined by three armoured cars from 6th LAMB.

On 12 June there was an action at Manjil Bridge which involved two cars from 6th LAMB, along with other troops. Manjil was on the road from Teheran to Resht. The bridge was covered by a force of 5,000 Jangalis – not a tribe as such, but the inhabitants of a nearby forested area – commanded by a pro-Bolshevik adventurer named Kuchik Khan. Outflanked by Bicharakov's Russians, the Jangalis fled and the two armoured cars raced forward to secure the bridge.

Later, on 2 July, British forces were in Resht, near the southern coast of the Caspian, when the town was attacked by some 2,500 Jangalis. Two armoured cars from 6th LAMB were with the British force, but many Jangalis rushed into the narrow streets of the town and made for the British Consulate, which they intended to sack. A company of Gurkha infantry and one armoured car effected a rescue. It took two days for the infantry and two armoured cars to clear the town.

By August 1918 two cars from 6th LAMB were in Zenjan with four Duncars Austins, anticipating a Turkish attack which never came.

Later in the year Dunsterforce, on the point of amalgamating with North Persia Force, was formed with four Rolls-Royces from 6th LAMB and what once was known as Duncars. It now consisted of 16 twin-turreted Austin armoured cars – not a patch on the Rolls-Royces but adequate for their role.

Khan Baghdadi, on the south bank of the Euphrates and almost due west of Baghdad itself, was the next objective for General Brooking in March 1918. He had under his command the 11th Cavalry Brigade of Brigadier-General Cassels, which included 13th and 14th LAMBs with a total of 13 armoured cars and the Mobile Column commanded by Lieutenant-Colonel J. Hogg which included 8th LAMB. Under pressure from London, the Army in Mesopotamia was starting to appreciate the value of armoured cars as a hard-hitting mobile element and they were gradually gaining a higher profile in operations. In this case they were sent along the Aleppo Road at 3.30am on 26 March with instructions to attempt to get around the enemy's right flank, to attack his rear and prevent him from departing. By 4.30am they were on the Aleppo Road facing south-east and firing into the Turkish right and rear. The Turks attempted to break through but were driven back and captured. Sir T.R.L. Thompson (7th Hussars), commanding the Light Armoured Car Brigade, now sent 11 cars from 13th and 14th LAMBs (the other two were escorting transport) along the Haditha Road and rounded up 2,000 prisoners. Six cars from 13th LAMB went somewhat further, looking for more.

Meanwhile, 8th LAMB, under Hogg, were sent to take Haditha, where they were reinforced by the other cars of General Cassels' force, and were directed towards Ana, even closer to Aleppo. Arriving at Ana, which the Turks had prudently evacuated, they learned that two British prisoners they also had orders to look out for, Lieutenant-Colonel J.E. Tennant, Royal Flying Corps and Major P.C.S. Hobart, Royal Engineers, who had been shot down while flying over Turkish lines, had passed through Ana on 27 March with their Tartar escort en route to Aleppo. The cars gave chase and although the rescue is sometimes credited to 13th LAMB, the preferred claimant is Captain Tod, commanding 8th LAMB. He is said to have spotted the party some 32 miles beyond Ana, to have chased off the escort and rescued the two prisoners, one of whom, Hobart, went on

to command 79th Armoured Division during the Second World War.

But that was not the end of their adventures. The cars went on for another 18 miles before turning back. They were looking for a hoard of 18,000 golden Liras, a part-payment by the Germans to Sheik Ajaimi of the Muntafik, whom they hoped would fight on their side. There were those who thought the money was a bit of a chimera but on 29 March 13th LAMB was sent a further 73 miles beyond Ana looking for it. They had no more luck. It will be noted that as the Mesopotamian force was moving west it was getting closer to places such as Aleppo, which more properly belong to General Allenby's campaign in Palestine. This is because both armies were slowly coming together, pushing the Turks out of territories they had occupied for years and back into their homeland. The end of the war with Turkey was in sight.

In late April 1918 another offensive was launched against Turkish positions in Kurdistan. The attacking force had been organised into columns A to D; Column A included 8th and 13th LAMBs. They came up against a Turkish position east of Kulawand on the morning of 27 April and as usual the armoured cars, supported by troops with Lewis guns in Model T Fords, attempted an outflanking manoeuvre on the right. However, they came to the edge of a swamp which the armoured cars could not cross. The position was nevertheless taken with a cavalry attack and the armoured cars were sent out along the road to Kifri seeking fugitives, though only a few were collected. On the next morning, 28 April, Column A sent the 13th Hussars with 'some armoured cars' on a reconnaissance along the road to Tuz Khurmatli. By that night 8th and 13th LAMBs were positioned to the right of Kulawand with a section of 14th LAMB with Column B1 about 6 miles away to the west. At about 10.15pm, 8th and 13th LAMBs were ordered to send some armoured cars to Tauq, but they came unstuck when they attempted to ford the Aq Su river. In fact it was the afternoon of the 29th before they got across; they had to be hauled through the water by artillery horses. Advancing on Tauq they then came up against the Tauq Chai river, where enemy troops on the far bank put up such a barrage of fire that the armoured

ABOVE Locally made Rolls-Royce armoured cars in India, parked up near a fort on the North-West Frontier.

BELOW The man standing beside the car is identified as Harry Denton, the dog's name is 'Stumps'. Notice the hinged cover for the lubrication tank on the side of the chassis, and the struts linking the dumb irons to the cross member – usually reckoned to be classic identification features of the Rolls-Royce.

cars were obliged to pull back. The next day, 30 April, while on a recce patrol, 8th LAMB discovered that the Turks had pulled out of Tauq.

Early in May, 8th and 13th LAMBs, now considered part of General Cayley's force, located a bridge over the Tauq Chai which the Turks had not destroyed. Advancing, they discovered the Turks in position in front of Taza Khurmatli on 3 May 1918. On 9 May, after a period of heavy rain, armoured cars made a reconnaissance towards Altun Kopri, while subsequent reconnaissances by armoured cars and other arms showed that Turkish forces were steadily withdrawing.

For the last few days of the war, from 27 October 1918 until the 31st when the Armistice with Turkey was signed, General Cassels directed a British force along the Tigris; 8th and 13th LAMBs, now acting as a Light Armoured Motor Brigade, led the way acting in the role of a reconnaissance unit, but there was very little action to report. In effect the war in the east was over.

India

Since, by its very location, India was a long way from the seat of war, the chances of any British armoured cars arriving there was very slim indeed. Yet India was an active front in its own right. The Russians were no longer a threat since they were now allies, but Afghanistan was seen as a risk as warfare among the tribes of the frontier regions was almost endemic and there were sporadic outbreaks of municipal violence in populated areas all over the country. With large numbers of experienced regular troops being called away to other theatres, those who replaced them were untried in the techniques of rigorous frontier warfare, and therefore armoured cars were regarded as one answer to the problem. Since it was impossible to obtain such vehicles from outside the country, the authorities in India, advised by Lord Montagu of Beaulieu and Captain Anthony Clifton of the Durham

LEFT This is 2641, which later became *Wedding Bells*, crossing a stream. It was an original machine-gun car with the bowed-out sides.

RIGHT Car No 2641 named *Wedding Bells*, acted as the bridal coach at the wedding of the adjutant of 1st Armoured Car Brigade. Here it is shown, slightly modified, parked alongside an Indian-pattern Crossley.

Light Infantry, decided to make their own. In 1915 private car chassis were donated by wealthy and patriotic individuals from all over the country or taken from dealers' showrooms and fitted with mild steel plate (since real armour was not available) at various railway workshops. Although there were exceptions, the majority were fitted with an open-top body, a door at the back and a totally enclosed engine compartment, while the radiator was either covered by louvres or by a pair of hinged doors. Clifton said that after firing a rifle at one he found that they were not bulletproof at all, but decided not to make this generally known. One out of every three cars was designated a machine-gun car; it had bowed-out sides so that the gunner could swing his weapon round, while the other two cars had flat sides and were seen as transport vehicles for riflemen.

LEFT As a few properly armoured cars arrived they gradually replaced the locally made ones. The first six came from the Middle East and were fitted with narrow normal air pressure (NAP) tyres (semi-solids) on disc wheels. This is 1st Armoured Motor Unit being paraded in Peshawar in about 1918.

LEFT Three Rolls-Royces lined up and ready to go although the location has not been identified. The rear doors to the fighting and driving compartments are open on each vehicle, waiting for the crews to board.

RIGHT Car No 8
with a bevy of senior
officers and an open-
top turret. This is the
only picture known to
exist that shows this
practice in India.

BELOW Rolls-Royce
Car No 9 with no gun
mounted and with the
rear doors, including
the small turret door,
partially open.

According to Clifton, who was put in charge of these armoured cars, they were organised (where possible) into groups of three, although even where they were of the same make they were never of the same model or year. Only three were Rolls-Royces, all on 40/50hp Silver Ghost chassis but built in different years. In practice the Rolls-Royces were the only ones with the stamina for the work; others broke down or proved unable to carry the weight.

The Rolls-Royces formed No 1 Armoured Motor Unit, based at Peshawar and commanded by Clifton himself. They saw plenty

RIGHT Surrounded by
local inhabitants, an
armoured car stops by
the roadside. It seems
to be completely alone
apart from the open
touring car pulling out
to pass it.

LEFT Escorting a convoy of motorised and animal transport in the Khyber Pass. The roads here were very good but extremely vulnerable to attack by militant tribesmen so armoured cars were considered necessary.

of action on the North-West Frontier and proved to be so trustworthy and reliable that, rather than using other makes, the Rolls-Royces were used all the time, with different crews. Indeed, as more weapons became available, all three cars in the unit mounted machine-guns.

By 1917 the authorities in Britain agreed to supply a dozen turreted Rolls-Royces, in groups of three, but were unable to deliver. Instead, six armoured cars, all Rolls-Royces, were sent from the Middle East and operated for a time out of Peshawar, working with Clifton's original three machines.

ABOVE As mentioned on page 55 *Wedding Bells* was later modified. The body was only scrapped in 1948 and there were plans at one time to ship it over to the Tank Museum, but nothing ever came of it.

LEFT A Rolls-Royce in Parachinar, another Army camp in North-West Frontier territory.

Chapter Three

The interwar years

'In view of the situation in Mesopotamia and the protection there of our detachments and women and children, it is thought that prospective buyers of Rolls-Royce cars would not object to a very short postponement of delivery in order to promote the safety of those mentioned above.'

Notice in *The Times*, September 1920

OPPOSITE 20 June 1935: a British Army Rolls-Royce armoured car outside the Royal Ulster Constabulary police station on York Street in Belfast following riots after an Orange Order parade. *(Photo by Fox Photos/Getty Images)*

LEFT Cars of 15th LAMB attached to NorPerForce (North Persia Force) carried extra spare tyres on top of the turret. This one has halted for some engine adjustment.

Aftermath of the First World War

The First World War may have ended but the fighting didn't, at least not in the Middle East. NorPerForce (North Persia Force) had been raised on 17 September 1918 under the command of Major General W.M. Thomson, which included surviving elements of Dunsterforce in addition to other units of the British Army in Persia. More particularly it included some cars from 6th LAMB, with two Rolls-Royces at Resht, two more at Zenjan with four ex-Duncars Austins and three more Austins at Hamadan. Meanwhile, Dunsterville himself had been recalled to India. Later these cars were replaced by those of 15th LAMB which was part of the force that reoccupied Baku in November 1918. Some of their cars were photographed among the oil wells at Baku, locally called volcanoes, but there is no indication of their actually doing anything besides undertaking security patrols.

The insurrection in Mesopotamia began in May 1921, at a time when large numbers of British troops and naval units could be

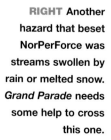

ABOVE An armoured car that appears to have been burned out, abandoned by the roadside on the route back through north Persia.

RIGHT Another hazard that beset NorPerForce was streams swollen by rain or melted snow. *Grand Parade* needs some help to cross this one.

LEFT Camouflaged Rolls-Royces of 6th LAMB at Al Mayadin on the Euphrates in January 1919. The second car from the camera has the larger turret.

BELOW The 1st Armoured Car Company, Tank Corps, in Persia or Iraq between May 1920 and December 1922. They are posing between two 1920-pattern Rolls-Royce armoured cars, but the crew would neither wear their sun helmets inside the vehicles, nor their best uniforms for everyday use.

seen leaving the country. It seems to have been caused by a rather high-handed British administration and a fear among the local inhabitants that Britain intended to annexe the country. The order of battle of the Mesopotamian Expeditionary Force included the 6th and 7th Light Armoured Motor Batteries and it was a section of four cars from one of these that was involved in the action at Tel Afar in June 1921. Tel Afar was an old town of narrow streets and steep hills which was described by Lieutenant-General Sir Aylmer Haldane (who commanded the Expeditionary Force) as a 'veritable death trap' for an armoured car. The section of armoured cars had arrived at the south-east corner of the town to suppress a supposed threat, but was warned in a message dropped from an aircraft that a large party of mounted men were approaching from the north-west. The armoured cars, led by the section commander, now penetrated the town with a view, it is thought, to rescuing any survivors in the civil buildings. They were ambushed by riflemen firing down from the tops of buildings in a particularly narrow street and all the crews

ABOVE In actual fact the company would probably consist of a mixture of 1920-pattern cars and the older 1914-pattern on new chassis, as shown here. Notice the lower turrets on the older cars (the two in the centre).

LEFT A 1914/1920-pattern car in service with 3rd Armoured Car Company, Royal Tank Corps, in Egypt. Supports for an experimental wireless aerial can be seen on the turret, but note the tripod for the Vickers machine-gun stowed on the running board and the acetylene spot lamp on the shelf behind the spare wheel.

RIGHT Two crew members of *Grey Knight*, which was serving with 15th LAMB in 1919. Notice how the turret and crew compartment have been clad in asbestos in an effort to insulate their interiors from the heat.

were killed. Sir Aylmer reported that the vehicles were later salvaged.

Haldane seems to have regarded the Rolls-Royces as useless for operating in Mesopotamia, notwithstanding the useful service they gave there during the war. He tells us that they were manned by infantry, suggesting that their original Machine Gun Corps crews had gone home. He also says that the cars were 'old and much the worse for wear', some indeed being unserviceable. As it was they could only muster sufficient crews to man two or three sections in a battery and rarely could more than four cars serve with a battery at any one time. Haldane sent for tanks instead, but was told that none were available. It was also discovered that in regions of cultivation, canals and irrigation ditches limited their mobility. Apparently the Arabs also developed a technique of shooting at the armoured car's pneumatic tyres to put them out of action.

In India eight more Rolls-Royces came from the Middle East when 13th Light Armoured Motor Battery was disbanded in Mesopotamia or Persia in 1919. In due course they were fitted with protected loopholes in the bevelled tops of their armoured turret roofs, through which rifles could be fired at tribesmen sniping from high vantage points in the passes.

Meanwhile, the machine-gun car (No 2641) from the original trio was sent to the Gun Carriage Factory at Jubbulpore to be fitted with a turreted body, apparently designed by some of Clifton's men. An angular turret was fitted, armed with a machine-gun, since the art of bending such thin plate was not known locally. Subsequently in 1921, when these cars were all enrolled into the Tank Corps, a new 7th Armoured Car Company was formed at Bovington and the men shipped out to India to take over the 14 turreted Rolls-Royces and the modified car which was originally named *Golden Goblin* but was renamed *Wedding Bells* in 1920, having officiated at a military wedding. Although the normal establishment of a Tank Corps Armoured Car Company was 16 vehicles, 7th ACC never seems to have had more than 15.

The 1920-pattern cars

A list of chassis numbers compiled by the late B.T. (Terry) White will be used here for want of anything better.

Of the 1920-pattern cars it shows 100 chassis (101 WO to 200 WO) delivered in November 1920, with a further 40 delivered in batches in 1921: 220 WO to 231 WO in March, 232 WO to 235 WO in September and 236 WO to 259 WO in October. At least 21 of these were completed as 1924-pattern armoured cars, but since they all used the 40/50hp Silver Ghost chassis they were indistinguishable at this stage. A further three were delivered in October 1927 but since Silver Ghost production

LEFT The classic 1920-pattern Rolls-Royce had Michelin disc wheels and the higher-sided turret, which distinguished it easily from the 1914-pattern. At first, ditch-crossing boards were stowed vertically on each side; later, when horizontal running boards were added, the ditch-crossing boards were stowed underneath.

ABOVE What is believed to be a detachment from 12th Armoured Car Company. The cars are named *Eileen II, Elijah, Ezra* and *Emily*. All are painted a light colour. Notice the lower set of the headlamps, no longer mounted on the mudguards.

LEFT A pair of 1920-pattern cars on a reconnaissance patrol down a country lane. The turret marking suggest the HQ Section.

ended in 1925 these may have been on the new Phantom 1 chassis which was almost identical but with a slightly taller engine. These three (277 WO to 279 WO) were definitely completed as 1924-pattern cars on contract V/1628 issued on 27 August 1927 and issued with WD numbers T406 to T408.

In 1921 we have a batch of 19 chassis – WO 201 to WO 219 – supplied to the India Office, followed by four chassis (266 WO to 269 WO) sold to the Persian government and delivered in November and December 1923.

The Royal Air Force is listed as taking

LEFT A Rolls-Royce of 3rd Battalion negotiates a ford on a lane near Salisbury in Wiltshire. There is an officer standing in the back, although the driver's visor is closed down.

LEFT A whole line of armoured cars, probably an entire company, halted on a country lane. The letter 'A' in red on the side of the leading car indicates a combat vehicle.

delivery of 13 chassis. Six (260 WO to 265 WO) were ordered on 14 March 1922 and delivered on 31 March 1922, and seven (WO 270 to WO 276) were ordered on 30 July 1927 and delivered to the Ascot Depot of the RAF in September and October 1927. Once again, given the date, this final batch may have been Phantom 1 rather than Silver Ghost chassis.

The story of the basic 1920-pattern car is a slightly complicated one, hedged about with myth and legend. According to one story the War Office approached the Admiralty for drawings of the wartime cars in order to design a new model for 1920. However, it is understood that the Admiralty used the Norwich firm Duff, Morgan and Vermont (Vermont was in fact the pseudonym of Oliver Locker-Lampson MP), who set up a drawing office in London but are said to have destroyed all their drawings by 1918. Thus it seems the War Office had to start from scratch, although they knew which chassis was to be used: the Rolls-Royce 40/50hp Silver Ghost and a 1914-pattern armoured car would be available for measuring. The cars were built by the Ordnance Factory at Woolwich, with 8mm-thick armour plate covering the engine, crew compartment and turret. Wood was used behind the crew compartment to form a hinged tailgate and two stowage lockers over the rear wheels. Features that singled these cars out are the armoured ventilation louvres in the radiator

doors. The raised vision slit on the driver's side of the hinged flap at the front of the crew compartment seems to have been required to accommodate a repositioned steering wheel, so that the driver could see over the top of the wheel. The slit on the other side was lower. The turret was also somewhat taller to provide more internal headroom than in the 1914-pattern cars. The turret was rotated entirely by hand; there were no mechanical aids at all such as a geared system, only handles bolted to the vertical turret walls. The turret rotated on three rollers located equidistant around the perimeter,

BELOW An armoured car, rather over burdened with camouflage vegetation, makes its way down the road. One hopes the driver can see where he's going.

though it could also be lowered into a fixed position for firing.

The 1920 Silver Ghost chassis, which was also fitted to some reworked 1914-pattern cars, had the front wheels covered by firm, more stylish mild steel mudguards which supported the sidelights. They ran on Michelin steel disc wheels, double at the back, but originally had no running boards since they were not really necessary. Instead the two detachable unditching boards were stowed on edge, one on each side. Later on, horizontal running boards were fitted and the unditching boards, also now horizontal, slotted in underneath.

Tank Corps/Royal Tank Corps Armoured Car Companies, of which 12 were raised after the First World War (at least those operating in the British Isles and the Middle East), consisted of 16 Rolls-Royce armoured cars, organised into 4-car sections. To begin with they were a mixture of 1914-pattern and new 1920-pattern vehicles, latterly the former were modernised by fitting the bodies on to more modern chassis and in this form they served alongside the more modern cars for many years.

In March 1921 began a General Strike, better known as the Miners' Strike, which lasted for about six weeks. On Friday 15 April 1921 the railway and transport workers were supposed to join in, but their union leaders decided not to call them out. The day became known as 'Black Friday' in union circles. Over 600 Tank Corps reservists were mobilised and temporary armoured car companies were raised and stationed at railway centres all around the country but the types of armoured car involved, which must have included some Rolls-Royces, is not described. In 1923 eight Yeomanry regiments were mechanised and nominated as armoured car companies of the Territorial Army, as follows:

- 19th Armoured Car Company (Lothian and Borders Horse)
- 20th Armoured Car Company (Fife and Forfar Yeomanry)
- 21st Armoured Car Company (Royal Gloucestershire Hussars)
- 22nd Armoured Car Company (Westminster Dragoons)
- 23rd Armoured Car Company (3rd County of London Yeomanry, The Sharpshooters)
- 24th Armoured Car Company (Derbyshire Yeomanry)
- 25th Armoured Car Company (Northamptonshire Yeomanry)
- 26th Armoured Car Company (East Riding of Yorkshire Yeomanry).

BELOW A 1914-/1920-pattern car in Royal Tank Corps service, stuck in the sand. Notice that dual wheels have also been fitted to the front axle to reduce ground pressure, but they must have made it hard work to steer.

LEFT His Majesty's Armoured Car (HMAC) *Chatham* of 1st Armoured Car Company, Tank Corps, in Mesopotamia. The wireless equipment and aerial were installed by the Royal Air Force (RAF) for ground-to-air communication when on patrol, one of the main factors that led to the formation of the RAF's armoured car companies.

Each unit had two armoured cars – not always Rolls-Royces – on permanent establishment and drew more from a reserve pool, with regular Army drivers, for exercises. Rolls-Royce armoured cars were also kept at Bovington, home of the Royal Tank Corps Depot Battalion, for training and ceremonial parades.

Another General Strike began on 1 May 1926. Most of the armoured car companies sent to London to escort food convoys from the docks were equipped with Peerless vehicles, but one section of Rolls-Royces, hastily drawn together by the Royal Tank Corps Schools at Bovington, was sent to Chelsea Barracks along

BELOW Armoured car *Kurdistan* in Tank Corps service. It has the extra top to the turret but the new chassis, characterised by disc wheels.

Third Battalion Royal Tank Corps was based at Lydd in Kent. In 1927–28 at the time of the great exercises on Salisbury Plain they adopted a disruptive camouflage scheme and provided the reconnaissance element, which is why, in addition to a Mark II Medium Tank, they have 1920-pattern Rolls-Royce armoured cars, two-man Morris-Martel tankettes and Carden-Loyd Mark VI Carriers.

with a medium tank company from 2nd Battalion for the duration of the strike which ended on 12 May. At the same time 12th Armoured Car Company, then stationed in Belfast, was moved across to Warrington in Cheshire and remained there after the strike was over.

A section of Rolls-Royces belonging to 12th Armoured Car Company was sent to Wiesbaden in Germany in January 1926 at about the same time as C Company, 3rd Battalion, Royal Tank Corps, left Cologne, it being the last British tank unit doing occupation duties in Germany. Now only the armoured cars remained. Then, on 31 March 1929 12th Armoured Car Company was disbanded and cars belonging to the section then in Germany were handed over to 3rd Battalion which, at the time, was stationed at Lydd in Kent. The remainder of 12th Armoured Car Company, upon disbandment, handed their armoured cars over to the 11th Hussars (Prince Albert's Own), one of the first two British cavalry regiments to be mechanised.

In the meantime, the Experimental Mechanised Force had been formed to operate on Salisbury Plain. Among those mustered for the event was 3rd Battalion, Royal Tank Corps, commanded by Lieutenant-Colonel F.A.

(Tim) Pile, which provided the reconnaissance element for the force. This consisted of two companies of Rolls-Royce armoured cars, one company of two sections, each consisting of four vehicles and one company of three sections of four cars, making twenty cars in all along with one section of tankettes (Morris-Martel and Carden-Loyd). Pile handled his part of the force boldly. The last exercise of the season was a mock battle, with elements of the Mechanised Force starting out from Micheldever in the east against a regular force moving from Andover in the west. With his armoured cars, taking advantage of their speed, Pile had most of the bridges over the rivers south of Salisbury 'captured' and blocked before the slow-moving traditional force could reach them. As a result, they were held up by armoured cars and tankettes until the tanks arrived to complete their destruction.

The force was mustered again the following year with roughly the same composition, but was now entitled the Experimental Armoured Force. Rather than engaging in another mock battle, it was mostly concerned with vehicle movement and tactical exercises. The force was disbanded once the event was over, never to be re-formed.

Armoured cars in India

Armoured cars had proved so successful during the war that the Indian government decided to continue with them afterwards. However, in the meantime the Tank Corps had been assigned the task of operating armoured car companies in India, from about 1920 onwards. The men were raised and the units trained at Bovington or Wareham and then

ABOVE Jamrud Fort at the head of the Khyber Pass. The leading car is a Rolls-Royce, rebuilt locally from one of the original cars and later to be known as *Wedding Bells* (see page 55). Following is a regular 1914-pattern car with a raised turret roof that served with 13th LAMB in the Middle East and came to India in 1919 when 13th LAMB was disbanded.

BELOW An unidentified 7th Armoured Car Company (ACC) Rolls-Royce in a North-West Frontier landscape. The fact that it has disc wheels and NAP tyres should indicate that it was one of the original six turreted cars sent to India in 1917.

ABOVE Driving up as close to the Afghan border as one could get seems to have been a popular thing to do with important visitors, but it was forbidden to cross. How this car came to be named *Black Viper* is uncertain.

shipped out to India, although there were not always armoured cars waiting for them when they arrived. Many of those used during the war were falling to bits and new ones were few and far between. In discussion with the Tank Corps the Indian government decided to acquire some new ones – Rolls-Royces, naturally, since they had already proved reliable. A.J. Clifton (now Major Clifton), in overall command of the armoured cars in India, was charged with going to Britain to order them. He sailed in 1920 and his other job while in Britain was to chase up the six vehicles they had been promised earlier but which had never arrived. He was also to investigate transport requirements. What Clifton discovered when he arrived was that new Silver Ghost chassis, prepared for military use, now

cost £2,100 each and bearing in mind that this was without the armoured bodies, he could only afford a limited number, settling finally upon a total of 19. In the meantime, he was invited down to Bovington to discuss the missing vehicles and when he got there discovered that a special demonstration had been laid on. The authorities had decided that Peerless armoured cars, of which they had a sufficiency, would do for India. The car duly appeared, driven by an accomplished Tank Corps driver, and described figures of eight and circles on the concrete hardstanding in front of the assembled visitors. Clifton was suspicious and requested the car be driven across some soft sand, where it immediately got stuck. After taking the wheel himself, Clifton declared that the heavy, solid-

RIGHT AND FAR RIGHT Front and rear views of A2645, a 1914-pattern car in virtually mint condition, but serving with 7th Armoured Car Company.

RIGHT Snow in the high country of the North-West Frontier was expected every winter and the Razmak plateau where the British built one of their most isolated camps was quite high up. Features to note, in addition to the disc wheels and NAP tyres, are the covered loopholes cut in the bevels of the turret roof. They could be used for firing rifles upwards if one was ambushed in a pass.

tyred Peerless was entirely unsuitable for India and turned it down, which made him very unpopular. In due course eight more war-weary Rolls-Royces went to India from the Middle East, but none would be coming from Britain. Because of this India ended up with a total of 14 Rolls-Royces, all 1914-pattern versions. No 1920-pattern cars ever went there. These older Rolls-Royces served with 7th Armoured Car Company for most of the interwar years. On these Indian Rolls-Royces, rifle loopholes in the turret bevels – for firing upwards in the passes – were a common feature.

When ordering the new chassis, Clifton specified that they should be fitted with steel disc wheels and with narrow Macintosh normal air pressure (NAP) tyres. These were

RIGHT *Silver Snipe* is another 1914-pattern car in original condition, except for the stowage on the running board.

LEFT Two armoured cars, one fitted for wireless, come up against a road block made from stones, in this case we hope, not a real one. It would be enough to stop an armoured car, although in this case it should have been possible to pass around the end of it – if you could do so without tumbling off the road.

ABOVE Fording a river, an Indian-pattern Rolls-Royce takes the plunge. This car is also camouflage-painted, including even the front mudguards and the commander's head cover.

two armoured car chassis into a comparative military hillclimbing trial on the North Downs, including the ascent at Leith Hill, which was a difficult climb thought to be similar to the type of terrain found in India. Far from winning the competition, the two Rolls-Royces failed miserably, Clifton blaming the gear ratios and the use of Rolls-Royce staff drivers who had no experience of that sort of thing. Others since then have suggested that the choice of wheels was to blame. Sir Henry Royce offered a solution involving a two-speed epicyclic final drive which would have cost a further £600 per vehicle, but this was more than Clifton could afford so the original order had to stand.

Clifton had the armoured bodies made by Vickers Ltd, who were glad enough to get military work in peacetime. Vickers decided to build them at their Erith factory in Kent, which they had acquired with Nordenfelt, and they put Sir George Buckham in overall charge. First a mock-up was built on a Rolls-Royce chassis, but on the actual vehicles 8mm-thick armour covered the entire car, even over the rear axle. So there was no open platform at the back as there was on cars serving in Britain. Another useful innovation was that the side doors were hinged to open different ways; the one on the left side opened forwards, while that on the right swung backwards. The idea was that anyone dismounting under fire could do

effectively solids but with triangular air pockets on the circumference which gave an element of cushioning – if they didn't fill with mud, that is. Rolls-Royce themselves weren't very keen on them and the manufacturers in turn were not happy that they could cope with such heavy vehicles (they weighed about 5 tons fully armoured). But pneumatic tyres did not last very long in Indian conditions, even when in store, while the NAP tyres, although liable to lead to skidding and overturning, lasted quite well. Rolls-Royce were cajoled into entering

RIGHT HMAC *Roedeer* armed and ready for action. Despite the fact that the prototype chassis put up such a poor show in England the cars seem to have been as good as any on the North-West Frontier. They were certainly more powerful than the numerous and similar-looking Crossleys.

so in relative safety, no matter which direction fire was coming from. There were also double doors at the back, and the interior was lined with Raybestos, a woven asbestos material designed to keep the heat down inside. The dome-shaped turret was an unusual design and almost unique to India. It is said to have been designed by Clifton himself. The rounded surface was intended to deflect bullets from any direction, especially from above, and four machine-gun positions were provided, two facing to the front and the other two at the back. Each car carried two machine-guns (the water-cooled Vickers .303), and they could either be mounted with both pointing in the same direction or one in each direction on opposite sides. It was claimed that a gun could be removed from a mounting and set up in another one in 15 seconds and a bulletproof cover, spring loaded, would snap into place whenever a gun was withdrawn. The turret was surmounted by an independently rotating clamshell-like cupola for the car's commander.

The new armoured cars arrived in India in

ABOVE Many Rolls-Royces lasted into the Second World War, but not with their original units. These cars are with the Calcutta and Presidency Battalion, a volunteer unit. Three are still in 1917 condition, with their disc wheels and NAP tyres, but the car on the far end named *Markhor* has War Department split rims and heavy-duty, broad-section tyres.

LEFT Another North-West Frontier scene near a typical village. The armoured car appears to have the name *Admain* painted across the back of the turret but what that means we do not know.

September 1922 and were issued to the 9th Armoured Car Company; 16 were used with two extras retained as spares, while the 19th car seems to have been sent to Ahmednagar as a reference vehicle.

Four more cars, almost identical to the dome-turreted Indian vehicles, were built by Vickers Ltd, and sold to the Persian (Iranian) government in 1923. The list of chassis numbers, already recorded, includes a note in parentheses saying that they were used by the RAF – though this seems unlikely, there being no record of it. The four cars only differ from those supplied to India in that they ran on pneumatic tyres, double at the back, with ordinary disc wheels and two spares are carried on the left side of the car.

The legend of their service with the RAF may have something to do with another story that we are unable to verify. The story is that an NCO and some men came across four Rolls-Royce armoured cars which were found in Persia, in near derelict condition, having been damaged to some extent with a hammer. The party of men got them all running again, drove them south to the Persian Gulf and offered them to the RAF, who supposedly did not want them.

Armoured cars in Ireland

After the end of the First World War, in December 1918 17th (Armoured Car) Battalion, Tank Corps, was moved hastily from Germany to Ireland. They arrived in Dublin in January 1919. A Company had 16 Austin armoured cars, B Company had 16 Medium A Whippet tanks and C Company had Mark IV tanks, later replaced by some Mark V* and Medium B tanks. In March 1920, 17th Battalion was disbanded and became No 5 Armoured Car Company, still with the same equipment. They were supplemented by some of the stately Peerless cars which were used for escorting lorry convoys and patrolling towns – in which roles they certainly impressed the locals; however, they were too heavy and slow and could not operate in the countryside, where the weary old Austins were used instead. In January 1921 it was decided to replace the Austins with new 1920-pattern Rolls-Royces that had been earmarked for Mesopotamia.

To begin with, under the overall control of 3rd Battalion, Tank Corps, a cadre unit, the armoured vehicles in Ireland consisted of 70 Peerless, just 2 Rolls-Royce armoured cars and 10 tanks, but these were scattered

at various locations throughout the country. More new Rolls-Royces arrived, direct from Woolwich, at which time many of the older cars were withdrawn, until there were enough vehicles to equip two four-car sections, one in Cork and one in Dublin. The main problem at first was finding suitable crews for them. Being more fast and mobile, the Rolls-Royces were used for escort and patrol work and raids in conjunction with Auxiliary Cadets of the Royal Irish Constabulary. The most effective operation, towards the end of this time, involved the Dublin section, in a counter-attack on the Customs House in Dublin which had been taken over by the IRA and which they were attempting to destroy. The speedy arrival of the armoured cars forestalled this and so many casualties were inflicted that an IRA battalion was effectively destroyed.

A truce was agreed in July 1921, following which the Irish Free State was created. Ulster, in the north, remained affiliated to the British Crown. Following this a civil war broke out, which British forces kept out of as much as possible. In April 1922 No 12 Armoured Car Company arrived, having been formed at Wareham in July 1921. It was equipped with 16 Rolls-Royce armoured cars but spent most of

its time defending the Ulster border. Meanwhile, No 1 Section of 5th Armoured Car Company was involved in breaking up what were in effect two IRA flying columns in June 1922.

On 17 December 1922 a huge convoy of British military vehicles left Dublin for Belfast: the evacuation of the Irish Free State had begun. Arms, equipment and vehicles had been handed over to the National Army from April 1922 and this ultimately amounted to over 1,000 vehicles including 13 Rolls-Royce armoured cars, 7 Peerless armoured cars and 111 armoured Lancia lorries. However, some Rolls-Royces, notably 185 WO *The Big Fella* and 161 WO *Custom House* were in National Army service around the time of the attack on the Four Courts in June and July 1922. The car 101 WO (originally known as *Danny Boy,* later as *Tom Keogh*), was involved in a number of actions against the 'Irregulars' as they were called, in Limerick and Kerry; one in particular near Kilworth Camp involved the car breaking through three columns of troops and then steering around barricades and crossing a partially destroyed bridge to reach safety. The car 103 WO, the preserved *Sliabh na mBan*, is famed as it was the car that was escorting Michael Collins, head of the provisional

BELOW A posed photograph of a Rolls-Royce in Ireland. The men are all badged Tank Corps and wear side arms, while the officer has a tank crew arm badge on his sleeve. Since each armoured car would probably carry a crew of three there is likely a second vehicle just out of sight, with the sixth man taking the photograph.

RIGHT When the British Army left southern Ireland they handed over 13 armoured cars to the Free State Army. Each one was named – this one is called *The Manager* – although the name does not appear on the original list. Note the soldier in the back who is armed with a Thompson sub-machine-gun.

LEFT Two more Irish armoured cars, *The Big Fella* and *The Fighting 2nd*. The group includes Major-General Tom Ennis.

government, when he was ambushed and killed at Beál na mBláth in August 1922. When they came under fire, the armoured car was unable to shoot back but Michael Collins dismounted from his staff car and joined in the gunfight until he was hit and killed. The armoured car itself is said to have been captured by the IRA but, being unable to use it, the car was hidden on a farm, minus its turret which was dumped in a muddy pond but later recovered. An entry in *A Short History of the Royal Tank Corps* states that two Peerless armoured cars were handed over in September 1922 along with two Rolls-Royces in November, although it is impossible to reconcile that.

By the time the convoy from Dublin arrived in Belfast, 12th Armoured Car Company was established in the city. The 5th Armoured Car Company moved to Scarborough in March 1923 but 12th Armoured Car Company

LEFT Rolls-Royce armoured cars were also used by the Royal Ulster Constabulary and, like those in the south, they secured the bonnet with a chain for additional security.

remained in Belfast until May 1926 when they were sent across to Warrington in Cheshire at the time of the General Strike. The British Army seems to have maintained a large stock of reserve vehicles on an airfield at Gormanstown, Co. Meath, in the Irish Free State. It must have included some Rolls-Royce armoured cars since six were duly handed over to the Royal Ulster Constabulary at about the same time and they were used for border patrols during the Second World War, often while similar cars belonging to the Irish Army were patrolling on the other side. During this time cars from both sides flew their own national flags.

The Irish Army retained its Rolls-Royce armoured cars until April 1954, although they were already experiencing difficulties with replacement tyres. The armour was removed and the chassis sold on for private use. Now just one armoured car remains, 103 WO *Sliabh na mBan*, which is preserved in full running order.

In Britain again

At a bridging demonstration held in the Sandhurst/Camberley area, probably over a stretch of the Basingstoke Canal, an armoured car was involved. By way of a preliminary, a Rolls-Royce armoured car advanced to cross a damaged bridge by means of its own bridging planks. (Since one could not go about damaging bridges in the English countryside just for a military demonstration, the bridge was probably intact, with the gap marked on it, perhaps in chalk.) The car approached the bridge, as if on a scouting mission, but was halted by the gap. Members of the crew dismounted and slid the two planks out from under the running boards

before placing them over the 'gap' in line with the vehicle's wheels. The driver then drove the armoured car gingerly across before the planks were retrieved and stowed in their rightful place and the car went on its way.

One of the problems with the Rolls-Royce unditching planks was that, in order to fit where they did, they were really too short, at less than 10ft long. The Experimental Bridging Establishment at Christchurch (then in Hampshire, now in Dorset) devised a special armoured car bridge in light alloy which was intended to be slung from the front

BELOW Rolls-Royces of 1920- and 1924-patterns take part in a parade of vehicles on Camberley Common on a wet day in November 1926. Ahead of them are two Peerless armoured cars. The event was the Dominion Premiers Display, which was attended by Winston Churchill among others.

RIGHT A section of armoured cars belonging to 12th ACC was sent from Belfast to Wiesbaden in Germany in January 1926 on Occupation duties, the only armoured car unit in the country. In March 1929, 12th ACC was disbanded so administration of the cars was taken over by 3rd Battalion, but soon afterwards Occupation duties ceased and the remaining tanks and armoured cars were shipped home. The photograph shows a Rolls-Royce being lifted aboard ship.

RIGHT Lessons on a Rolls-Royce at Bovington. A 1920-pattern car near the railway from Wool.

of the vehicle, either the armoured car itself or an accompanying lorry. Two lengths were developed: 27ft for a six-wheeled Lanchester armoured car and 10ft for a Rolls-Royce. For the Rolls-Royce, since this was hardly any longer than the planks carried by the vehicle itself, there was probably no great advantage and nothing more was ever heard of either design. However, during the Second World War the Royal Engineers were able to deploy track bridges, either 12ft or 20ft long, which fulfilled the same purpose.

Armoured car, Rolls-Royce, 1924-pattern Mark I

The prototype of the new 1924-pattern Rolls-Royces appeared towards the end of the year. It was distinctly different from the earlier version, with a longer bonnet, a new style of turret and the armoured body, with a door on the near side, continued all the way back, enclosing the entire chassis. The turret was taller than on the 1920-pattern cars and appears to have been of slightly smaller diameter. It lacked the side bevels

RIGHT Unloading armoured cars from a train, possibly in Yorkshire, so this may have been connected with a Yeomanry regiment of the Royal Tank Corps, 26th ACC (the East Riding Yeomanry) for example.

which are characteristic of the earlier cars, but sloped down gradually at the front and had a short, steep bevel at the rear. A large oval cupola was provided on top, arranged crosswise, and the machine-gun was now fitted in a splashproof ball mounting at the front. Probably more a pilot model than a true prototype (since it still employed the well-known Rolls-Royce Silver Ghost chassis) the car was F341 (ME9945) and it was used by Colonel George Lindsay for a training run to South Wales, culminating in some hillclimbing trials around the Rhondda Valley.

Production cars, of which 24 were built by the Woolwich Ordnance Factory, were more or less the same but lacked the enclosed section at the back, probably to save weight. Instead they were fitted with an open section with wooden lockers on each side and a hinged tailgate at the back (as on the 1920-pattern cars, only shorter). Three of these cars (F406 to F408) were built to a contract dated 1927. Since Rolls-Royce stopped producing the Silver Ghost in 1925, these may have appeared on its replacement, the Phantom 1 chassis, which was essentially the same size but fitted with a more powerful engine. Either that or Rolls-Royce continued to turn out Silver Ghost chassis solely for the Army.

ABOVE The Mark IA was a rebuild of the 1920-pattern car to bring it into line with the new 1924-pattern vehicle. It can be recognised by the longitudinal cupola on top of the turret and, if you can see it, by the way the machine-gun fits into a ball mount, and splash deflecting strips on the bonnet top.

BELOW The prototype of the 1924-pattern Rolls-Royce had a longer armoured body along with the new design of turret. It was photographed in Pontypridd, South Wales. Colonel George Lindsay from Bovington travelled with it, intending to show it to one of his brothers, who was Chief Constable of Glamorgan.

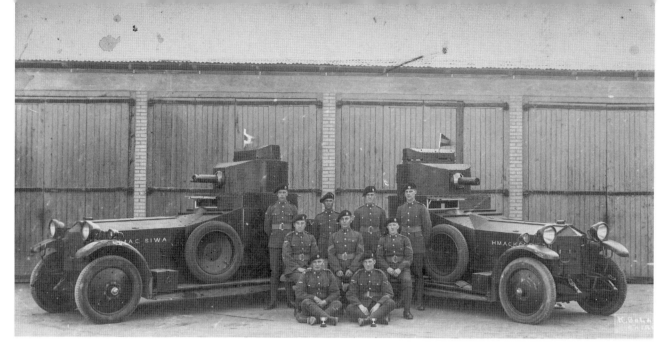

ABOVE Royal Tank Corps personnel posing with a pair of Rolls-Royce 1924-pattern armoured cars.

Initially these new Rolls-Royces ran on Michelin disc wheels, twin at the back and Palmer cord tyres, but latterly, especially in the desert, they were equipped with broad-section sand tyres and split-rim wheels, single all round.

Rolls-Royce, 1920-pattern Mark IA

Probably around 1925 some Mark I 1920-pattern cars were taken in hand for conversion to Mark IAs; the idea seems to have been to bring them up to the same standard as the 1924-pattern cars. The conversion included fitting an oval cupola lengthwise along the top of the turret, replacing the original forked machine-gun mounting with a splashproof ball mounting and attaching strips of angle iron as bullet-deflecting rails along the top of the bonnet.

We do not know exactly how many cars were converted, but certainly not all. A hand-written ledger at Bovington, dating from the beginning of the Second World War, lists 10 as against 42 of the Mark I types still in service. But this may not be the full picture.

RIGHT The classic 1924-pattern armoured car, with the machine-gun aperture blanked off. The acetylene spot lamp is mounted at the front, just below the electric headlamps. Note that when wider, heavy-duty tyres were fitted they were not double at the back, although the spare, on this side anyway, appears to be of the normal type.

LEFT Two 1924-pattern Rolls-Royces with the 11th Hussars along with a group of officers and the inevitable dog. Both cars are camouflaged and the machine-gun mounting can be seen in the one on the left, but the turret cupola is missing.

The Mechanical Warfare Experimental Establishment (MWEE)

Located at Farnborough in those days the Mechanical Warfare Experimental Establishment, which had previously gone under various other titles, was responsible for testing samples of all military vehicles in service with the British Army and a few from other institutions such as the Colonial Office and the Royal National Lifeboat Institute. Four Rolls-Royce armoured cars went to MWEE for trials but, with the exception of one case, we have no idea of what was involved. Of the four, two were 1920-pattern Mark Is and two were Mark IAs. No 1924-pattern cars went there as far as we know. The only vehicle for which we have a description was M271 (H2593), which also carried the General Staff number D6E1, making it effectively the representative car of the type.

It participated in the North Wales trials of May 1933, which were mainly concerned with hillclimbing. It had been fitted experimentally with a Rolls-Royce Phantom 1 engine rated at 100hp which was evaporatively cooled. In other words, the coolant was kept at boiling point, so the system worked on steam. The car was also fitted, for these tests, with a five-speed gearbox and the trials, we are told, were mostly concerned with cooling. Although the trials seem to have been successful, no other Rolls-Royces were ever modified in this way and in due course M271 (or F271 as it later

became) was returned to its original condition and seems to have lasted into the early years of the Second World War.

One other modification, entailing a car with no visible numbers or registration mark, is known from photographs. It involves an armoured car mounting an air-cooled version of the Vickers machine-gun; the weapon retains the outer jacket seen on water-cooled weapons but with ventilation slots cut into it. It looks like an adaption from a water-cooled gun since all the associated fittings are in place but given that it was never seen again one assumes that it was not terribly successful. Since the water-cooled gun is never seen with the plumbing or the condenser in place, we can surmise that it was fired without it, and topped up as required. It may have been thought that an air-cooled weapon would work just as well, although apparently it didn't.

Overseas again – the Far East

In January 1927, 5th Armoured Car Company, Royal Tank Corps, was shipped out to China as part of the Shanghai Defence Force along with other British units sent from India. The company, commanded by Major A.H. Caldecott, took all 16 Rolls-Royce armoured cars with it and went in two ships, the SS *Karmala*, which sailed from London, and the SS *Bellerophon*, which left from Birkenhead. The eight cars stowed aboard the *Karmala* were lowered into a hold in such a way that every

LEFT No matter where they are, soldiers love posing for photographs. This one features a Rolls-Royce of 5th ACC in Shanghai in 1927. The car is fitted with a 'Top Hat' commander's lookout and a front bumper to fend off pedestrians.

car was accessible during the voyage, batteries could be kept topped up and engines turned over from time to time. On the *Bellerophon,* on the other hand, the cars were arranged around the edge of the hold with two mobile workshops in the middle and then a few tons of fodder were dumped on top. This meant that nobody could get near the cars during the voyage so no maintenance could be done. The *Karmala* docked in Shanghai on 9 March, and when the cars were unloaded they could be started and were ready for action at once, but when the *Bellerophon* turned up 13 days later, magnetos were damp, carburettors dirty and some pistons stiff with the added nuisance of the cars needing cleaning out as well; loose

LEFT Here, the Royal Tank Corps armoured cars in Shanghai are available for inspection by a select few.

BELOW In this photograph the other ranks are given a quick look while others wait with their rifles.

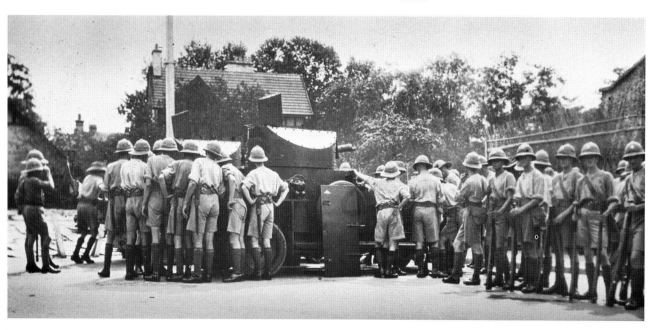

ABOVE However, most of the time they were on patrol around the city, being studied with passing interest by the locals.

RIGHT Another street scene from Shanghai providing an excellent view of the 'Top Hat' head cover hinged in the open position.

BELOW When not on patrol the armoured cars were kept in open sheds, watched over by a sentry.

on 21 March 1927 and involved two cars, one commanded by Lieutenant T.P. Newman, the other by Sergeant Tomlinson. Two machine-guns in the hands of rebel Chinese soldiers opened fire on the cars from a building on the corner of the street, and unable to manoeuvre while it was passing through barricades, Lieutenant Newman's car was struck 93 times, while the officer himself, when dismounting, was hit twice in the arm. Eventually the car was towed out of trouble by Sergeant Tomlinson's car, which had already silenced one machine-gun, though it required the services of the New Engineering Company to repair the damage. By January 1929 the 5th Armoured Car Company was ready to sail for home but in the meantime it conducted experiments with a lightweight version of the Indian Mat Bridge. This was carried (rolled up) in the back of an armoured car and unrolled over a local waterway, providing sufficient floatation to support men crossing on foot.

Mechanising the cavalry

1928 was a defining year for the British Army, for it was then announced that two cavalry regiments, the 11th Hussars and the 12th Royal Lancers, were to give up their horses and become mechanised, in this case with armoured cars. It was recognition, belated some might think, of what the First World War had already taught us: that the day of the mounted soldier was almost over. The two regiments had been chosen because they were the youngest, in historical terms, of those that had not already been amalgamated in the post-war reorganisation. Even so, both regiments could trace their history back to 1715 and all that time as part of the *arme blanche*, meaning those who use bladed weapons. The 11th Hussars were based at Tidworth on Salisbury Plain, while the 12th Lancers were at Helmieh near Cairo in Egypt. The 11th Hussars had mostly learned their new trade on the big, six-wheeled Lanchester armoured cars, but they left them behind in England; the 12th Lancers was mostly a Rolls-Royce regiment, having taken the cars over from 3rd and later 5th Armoured Car Companies, Royal Tank Corps, who not only taught them to drive, but also the particular skills associated with desert driving

TOP When the emergency in Shanghai was over, trials were undertaken with a floating bridge carried in the back of a Rolls-Royce.

ABOVE Here it is being launched; it was only intended for infantry and was only partially effective.

straw had got in everywhere. While they were in Shanghai a number of modifications were carried out; front bumpers were attached in case of accidents in the crowded streets and raised covers were fitted on top of the turrets to provide the commanders with a protected lookout. Work such as this, which was beyond the scope of the unit fitters, was done by the New Engineering Company in Shanghai. The lookouts, which were known as 'top hats', were hinged to fold backwards if the commander just needed to look from the top of the turret.

The cars had been sent because of the emergency caused by the advance towards Shanghai of the Cantonese Revolutionary Army under General Chiang Kai-Shek. This was threatening to disrupt life in the International Settlement, so detachments from the French Army and the United States Marine Corps were also present. Generally speaking, the presence of the armoured cars, simply patrolling the streets, was enough to prevent trouble and only one serious incident is recorded. This occurred

LEFT The 12th Royal Lancers, who preceded the 11th Hussars in Egypt, were the first to use the 1924-pattern cars out there; these are preparing for a desert expedition. Notice that the car on the end is finished in an unusual camouflage scheme.

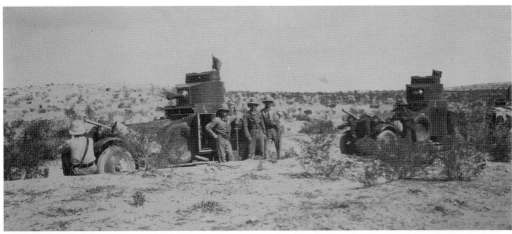

LEFT These cars are seen stopped during an expedition; extra stowage space seems to be at a premium.

that one needed in Egypt. The reconnaissance trip to Siwa Oasis in 1932, by a detachment from A Company, despite being made famous in the book *From Cairo to Siwa Across the Libyan Desert with Armoured Cars* by Major T.I. Dun, RAMC, was only one of many. Meanwhile, B Squadron, with nine armoured cars, was sent briefly to Palestine to deal with an outbreak of trouble and some time later a half-squadron was despatched to Cyprus to deal with rioting there.

Early in January 1935 the 11th Hussars, having replaced the 12th Lancers, mounted their first long-range reconnaissance trip into the Libyan desert. A Squadron went with ten Rolls-Royce armoured cars, a mixture of four- and six-wheeled transport, three Austin Sevens and some motorcycles. Their chosen destination was Baharia Oasis, some 200 miles away, but the majority of the trip would be across the open desert so it was a test of navigation skills linked to the difficulties of driving over the desert floor through a variety of conditions.

The armoured cars handled the conditions very well, but punctures affected the transport which also repeatedly got stuck in the soft sand. Meanwhile, the workshop lorries made heavy weather of the rough terrain. All this conspired to slow the entire convoy down. The trip out took a lot longer than expected, due as much to inexperience as anything else. Only the little Austin Sevens proved to be the ideal desert

BELOW Accidents will happen. What appears to be a 1920-pattern car has come off the road and turned over into a waterway.

ABOVE Mostly 1924-pattern cars halted at a desert fort. The only 1920-pattern car in the picture is ex-5th ACC, having been fitted with the 'Top Hat' in Shanghai.

LEFT A 1924-pattern car of the 12th Lancers in its garage with a large party draped over it to have their photograph taken.

RIGHT A 1920-pattern car of 12th Royal Lancers in Egypt. Formerly of 5th ACC in Shanghai, judging by the 'Top Hat' on the turret, it later passed to 3rd ACC and by them to the 12th Lancers, whom they trained in 1929.

BELOW A halt in the desert to let the cars cool down. Where the sand is hard it makes a good surface to drive on, but where it's soft and deep it can trap a car.

vehicles. Even the armoured cars became bogged down on at least one occasion, but the Austins never did. The journey back resulted in a number of mechanical breakdowns in addition to the other difficulties. At a point about 75 miles from Helmieh the armoured cars were given their heads and made it all the way home in one day, while the rest of the convoy limped slowly in some way behind.

Subsequently, similar long-range reconnaissance trips were carried out. Navigation improved and although the regiment was still a long way from being truly desert worthy, it was getting there. The Abyssinian Crisis of 1935 prompted by Mussolini now gave a new significance to the Libyan desert and in particular its long frontier with the Italian province of Cyrenaica, which was now marked by a tall barbed-wire fence. This gave added purpose to the presence of the British Army in the Libyan desert and a permanent base

was established at Mersa Matruh. Troops and armoured vehicles, however, were not permitted to go close to the frontier wire for fear of appearing provocative. Sollum was about as far forward as they were supposed to go. The 11th Hussars, the only armoured car regiment out there, spent most of its time at Mersa Matruh with a detached company at Sollum. In 1936 reinforcements arrived from Britain, including the 12th Royal Lancers, so for a while there were two armoured car regiments in Egypt, serving turn and turnabout in the desert.

Palestine

In April 1936 the Arab Rebellion broke out in Palestine; it too had its origins in Europe. Nazi persecution of the German Jews caused thousands of them to emigrate, while Britain, as the Mandatory Power, encouraged them to settle in Palestine – the Holy Land. Yet Britain,

ABOVE When they were stationed in Egypt, 11th Hussars were rushed out to Palestine in 1936 to help deal with an outbreak of violence. They were mostly equipped with 1924-pattern Rolls-Royces.

LEFT Rolls-Royces of 1920- and 1924-pattern with the 11th Hussars in Palestine, photographed on patrol.

BELOW This unamed armoured car running on heavy-duty tyres is a 1920-pattern Mark IA, without its cupola but with a Lewis gun on a Scarfe ring taken from an aircraft fitted instead. It was photographed at the edge of an airfield in Palestine; alongside the car is an aircraft signalling panel laid out on the ground.

due to its weak response to Italian aggression, had lost a lot of face with the Arabs. So the latest outbreak of the Arab Rebellion was directed as much against Britain as it was against the increasing numbers of Jews. The RAF, which was responsible for security in Palestine, could only field one company of armoured cars as ground troops so, in the summer of 1936, the 11th Hussars were sent out from Egypt. There they joined 6th Battalion, Royal Tank Corps, who had taken 18 Light Tanks Mark IIIs, but the tanks operated in the south while the 11th Hussars were sent up north. Here they served alongside No 2 Armoured Car Company, Royal Air Force, which was also equipped with Rolls-Royces. Indeed, it was from the RAF that the 11th Hussars learned to fit Lewis guns on stalks at the back of the turret. It involved removing the cupolas from the turrets of 1924-pattern cars, but

these were restored again and the Lewis guns removed when the regiment returned to Egypt in October 1936 after the worst of the rebellion was over.

While they were in Palestine the regiment was fully stretched – they had a lot of ground to cover. During the day they were escorting vulnerable convoys and at night patrolling the roads in company with hired civilian lorries mounting guns and searchlights taken from British warships stationed off the coast. These vehicles, known as *Pip, Squeak* and *Wilfred*, manned by Royal Navy crews and escorted by armoured cars, would go looking for improvised roadblocks covered by rebel riflemen who invariably melted away when they came under fire. This kind of activity became a popular pastime, so popular in fact that other members of the regiment, such as clerks and fitters, took it in turns to go along as armoured car crews.

LEFT A Hawker Hardy aircraft makes a mock attack and both the armoured car and the Commer Tender behind it are tracking it with their Lewis guns. Notice the RAF cockade painted on top of the turret as a recognition sign.

BELOW A mysterious picture showing four 1914/1920-pattern cars in 'as new' condition at No 1 Supply Depot, Kidbrooke, south-east London.

Rolls-Royces in the RAF

When the Tank Corps took over administration of armoured cars from the Machine Gun Corps in 1920 they organised them into Armoured Car Companies of sixteen vehicles and did so by absorbing eight-car Light Armoured Motor Batteries (LAMBs) and some four-car batteries as well. Thus when 1st Armoured Car Company, Tank Corps, was formed in Iraq in January 1921 it absorbed the cars of 6th and 15th LAMBs. Then, in June 1921 Lieutenant Colonel George Lindsay was sent out to Iraq with orders to create No 1 Group, Tank Corps, by combining 1st, 2nd and 6th Armoured Car Companies. At the same time, Lindsay experimented by sending the cars off on long-distance patrols supported, from the air, by the RAF. This was successful but it was proving expensive, so T.E. Lawrence (of Arabia), then serving as a political adviser to the Colonial Office, suggested to Sir Hugh Trenchard of the RAF that his service take over some of the armoured cars and operate them

RIGHT This 1920-pattern Mark IA car of No 2 ACC is being followed by a Rolls-Royce tender and other vehicles, while being overflown by a Westland Wapiti biplane.

RIGHT Three
1914/1920-pattern
cars in RAF service,
meeting up with a
flight of Westland
Wapitis in the desert.

in conjunction with aircraft instead. This came
to pass in 1922.

Since we know that the RAF started out with
48 armoured cars, we assume that it inherited
all the vehicles from No 1 Group, although it
seems by this time that some of the older cars
had been fitted with new chassis while others
had been replaced by new 1920-pattern cars.
Even so, No 2 Armoured Car Company, RAF, is
known to have had some original 1914-pattern
cars with wire-spoked wheels to begin with.
There is still a lot we don't know about the RAF
cars, but it seems that the early cars were all
fitted with new chassis in due course. Apart
from RAF roundels painted on the cars, most
of those in RAF service can be identified by the
Lewis gun mounted at the back of their turrets,
by the spotlamp at the front and the holders for
signal flags on the side bevels. In 1922 the RAF
acquired six new cars of their own; the chassis
came from Rolls-Royce while the armoured
bodies were built at No 1 Stores Depot at
Kidbrooke, London. They are said to have been
made from slightly thicker armour than the War
Office cars – making them somewhat heavier
and a bit slower – but they looked almost
identical except that the wooden lockers at the
back were larger. These vehicles were described
as Type A in RAF service, although there is no
indication of a Type B or anything else for that
matter. Then, in 1927, the RAF acquired seven
more cars. As this was some two years after
Rolls-Royce ceased to produce the Silver Ghost
chassis, these may have been the very similar

RIGHT Active was
a 1914/1920-pattern
Rolls-Royce carrying
the badge of 2nd ACC,
followed by a tender
that is also armed with
a Lewis gun.

Phantom 1. It is also possible that these cars were fitted with 1920 Mark IA bodies. We know the RAF had some, unless of course they came from the War Office. Subsequently the RAF transferred some armoured car bodies on to commercial Fordson lorry chassis. They looked very similar, as one might expect, but they were no longer Rolls-Royces.

Egypt again

By November 1936 the 11th Hussars and their Rolls-Royces were back at Helmieh again, looking forward to a lengthy period of what they termed 'peacetime soldiering'. There were military exercises of course and the regiment was involved in eight of them over the next two years. Once again, as the Arab Rebellion flared up in Palestine, the 11th Hussars were called back there to resume their old practices albeit in different places. They were, however, recalled urgently to Egypt, by land and sea, leaving B Squadron behind. This was the period of the Munich Crisis but once that was over and 'peace in our time' certain (for a while anyway) it was back to Palestine again only this time leaving behind a core of armoured car crews and their vehicles to continue training. In the aftermath of the Munich Crisis, Major-General P.C.S. Hobart had been flown out from Britain and appointed to the command of a new formation to be known as the Mobile Division (Egypt). The 11th Hussars, with two light tank regiments, formed the Light Armoured Brigade, although the Hussars, as the only armoured car regiment,

was (although not then complete) effectively the reconnaissance element for the entire division. They were summoned back to Cairo in April for another emergency and there was no further recall to Palestine. War was growing close. From Helmieh they ultimately drove out to Mersa Matruh and they were still there on 3 September 1939, when war was declared. Hobart, while retaining the division at Mersa Matruh, sent the armoured cars to the frontier to watch the Italians, but once it became clear that they had no immediate plans to move, the 11th Hussars were recalled to Mersa Matruh and in November the entire division went back to Cairo for Christmas. In the meantime Hobart had been dismissed by Wavell and for a while it looked as if his military career was ended.

Chapter Four

The Second World War

'The fighters must have reached
the limit of their fuel, for suddenly
they sheered off altogether. . . .
The 11th Hussars emerged from
their holes, somehow got the car
backed up on to a convenient
camel hump, and there the wheel
was changed. By 1pm the
Rolls-Royce, with guns
remounted, was on its way back
to Squadron Headquarters to
receive fresh orders.'

Gabr Saleh, Libya, 24 August 1940.
From *The Eleventh at War* by Brigadier Dudley Clarke

**OPPOSITE A 1924-pattern car with the 11th Hussars in the
Egyptian desert, with a modified turret made and fitted at the
Nairn Brothers workshops in Cairo. It mounts a Bren gun, a
Boys anti-tank rifle and a smoke bomb discharger and was
open at the top. The car is also fitted with a condensing tank to
conserve radiator water.**

At the outbreak of the Second World War in 1939 most of the Rolls-Royce armoured cars still in Britain were employed on home defence duties. This included patrolling the beaches on the east coast to give warning of any attempts at invasion and patrolling RAF aerodromes to deal with airborne invaders – either parachute troops or those landed in transport aircraft – and in some cases providing a few vehicles for newly raised armoured car regiments, pending delivery of something more up to date. In Ulster about a dozen cars were issued to the North Irish Horse when it became a Light Armoured Regiment (wheeled) on 31 August 1939, just before war was declared. The North Irish Horse was designated as a militia regiment in 1921 but was then effectively placed in suspended animation until 1939 when it was transferred to the Supplementary Reserve and incorporated into the Royal Armoured Corps. However, the vehicles were getting a bit long in the tooth and were duly replaced with Humber Light Reconnaissance Cars, although the regiment

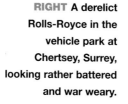

ABOVE A clear side view of the Home Guard Rolls-Royce. Two other Home Guard Rolls-Royces are known – one in Kent and another in East Lancashire.

RIGHT A derelict Rolls-Royce in the vehicle park at Chertsey, Surrey, looking rather battered and war weary.

ABOVE A pair of 1920-pattern cars with the North Irish Horse in Ulster – better than nothing, but only just.

LEFT The North Irish Horse on an exercise in 1939. Having been held in suspended animation since 1919, the regiment formed part of the Supplementary Reserve and became an armoured car regiment. It converted to tanks in 1940 and fought in Italy in Churchills.

later converted to tanks. Mention has already been made of the Rolls-Royce armoured cars of the Royal Ulster Constabulary which patrolled their side of the border during the Irish Civil War, matched by Rolls-Royces of the Irish National Army on the other side.

Armoured cars in North Africa with the 11th Hussars

The doyen of Rolls-Royce users at this time was the 11th Hussars, still stationed in Egypt and now equipped with a mixture of Rolls-Royce and Morris CS9 Light Armoured Cars. The Morrises, which were said to perform better on soft sand, were employed as troop leader's cars while the Rolls-Royces, which served as the other two cars in the troop, were 1924-pattern cars with modified turrets. These new turrets were high-sided open-top boxes that rested on the original turret ring so they could only be turned manually. The turrets were made and fitted at the workshops of the Nairn Transport Company in Cairo and were armed with a Boys .55-calibre, single-shot anti-tank rifle, a 4in smoke bomb discharger and a Bren light machine-gun, which was either mounted at the front alongside the other two or could be moved to the back of the turret and fitted to an anti-aircraft mounting. This armament placed them on a par with the Morris

vehicles, although the regiment recorded that the Bren gun, with its clip-on magazine, was not a very effective anti-aircraft weapon.

War with Italy began on 11 June 1940 and elements of the regiment were sent at once to the frontier with Cyrenaica to break through the fence in various places. A replica stretch of fence had been created at Mersa Matruh for the armoured cars to practise on and an effective method had been devised for breaking it down. They broke through in four places and made an aggressive foray into enemy territory. As time went by they got bolder and often camped there as well, until the Italians pulled all their front-line troops back.

For most of the rest of that summer the 11th Hussars seemed to have vast areas of the Italian desert to themselves. The Italians may have greatly outnumbered them but they had no armoured cars and most of their tanks were worse than useless. Their artillery was bravely handled, but it is not easy to shell a moving armoured car. The Italian air force was another matter, though. Fighter aircraft armed with machine-guns could do a lot of damage to

armoured cars and often set them alight; if they didn't manage that, they could tear the cars' tyres to shreds. Even bombers, if they could hit close enough, could be a menace. If the cars were stationary and well camouflaged they might be missed altogether, so long as nobody on the ground was moving around, but cars caught in the open, even under way, made for easy targets and were regularly harried from the air.

Then, on 7 October, the 11th Hussars received reinforcement. It came in the shape of No 2 RAF Armoured Car Company with ten Rolls-Royces commanded by Flight Lieutenant Casano, which formed a temporary D Squadron for the next four months or so.

Massing behind the frontier wire, Italian forces, under Marshal Rudolfo Graziani, began an advance into Egypt. While British forces remained behind their defences at Mersa Matruh, the 11th Hussars continued to conduct reconnaissance patrols, watching the advancing Italians along the various routes they had selected. The Italians got no further than Sidi Barrani, a good 60 miles short of Mersa Matruh, and there they settled down in a long line of defended camps leading south.

ABOVE This view of a modified Rolls-Royce of the 11th Hussars shows the vehicle up against the Italian wire at the Libyan frontier.

RIGHT Two Rolls-Royces of No 1 ACC, RAF, were knocked out at Antelat in Cyrenaica on 22 January 1942. Here, one of them is being commented on by Erwin Rommel, the German commander in North Africa.

The camps were so badly placed, however, that they were unable to support one another, with gaps between them so wide that British patrols could drive through and get behind them. The southernmost Italian camps were at Sofafi, on top of the escarpment.

The Battle of Sidi Barrani, which the British also called Operation Compass, took place over four days early in December 1940. It resulted in the evacuation of all the camps and an Italian retreat into Cyrenaica. The Hussars, with their armoured cars, were involved in a number of sweeps calculated to intercept as many enemy troops as possible. In all some 38,000 men surrendered, along with tons of *matériel*. When all the Italians still in Egypt had been rounded

RIGHT Another view of one of the Rolls-Royces with a 3.7in anti-aircraft gun in the background. Antelat, which was used by the RAF as a forward airstrip, was not far from Beda Fomm, site of the famous action in February 1941.

up, the British crossed the frontier again and began to probe around the fortified towns of Bardia and the port of Tobruk, but here they were visited again by Italian aircraft, notably a squadron specially dedicated to dealing with them that fired armour-piercing rounds and used low-flying tactics against the vehicles. A number of cars were lost or damaged in this way and several men were killed or wounded.

While the Australian 6th Division was forming up to attack Bardia, the armoured car regiment, further west, was capturing Italian airfields and trying to get their own back for some of the attacks they had suffered. They were only partially successful, though, because air attacks continued; it seemed to be the only way the Italians knew to counter the armoured cars. Some vehicles were hit, with men either killed or wounded, but since the 11th Hussars were operating as individual squadrons some suffered more than others. Bardia was taken and the Australians moved on to assault Tobruk, by which time the Hussars were deep in the desert. They were reconnoitring a route cutting south of the Jebel Akhdar in the hope of finding a direct route to the coast road south of Benghazi, where General O'Connor hoped to halt and capture the retreating Italian Army. In an effort to prevent this, Marshal Graziani attempted to block the road at Mechili with tanks and entrenched infantry. Since Britain did not have the tanks to deal with this, the armoured cars were ordered to find a route further south, but in the meantime Graziani decided to abandon Cyrenaica altogether. The force at Mechili was therefore ordered north, along a pass through the Jebel Akhdar, followed by the 11th Hussars. Since this cleared away the blockage at Mechili, the route to the west was now open. The 11th Hussars were recalled to scout ahead for the 7th Armoured Division, apart, that is, from B Squadron, which joined up with the Australians pursuing the Italian Army around the coast road.

As a result, elements of the 11th Hussars, led by C Squadron, were first to arrive on the road near Beda Fomm. Now known as Combeforce (after the regiment's commanding officer) this composed 2nd Battalion the Rifle Brigade, three batteries of Royal Horse Artillery and some armoured cars. Thus on 5 February 1941 a roadblock was formed south of Beda Fomm and,

pending the arrival of 4th Armoured Brigade, the only vehicles present were the armoured cars of the 11th Hussars, most of them ancient Rolls-Royces dating from 1924. There they met the head of the huge Italian column retreating from Cyrenaica towards Tripolitania, who were very surprised to find that the Hussars had got there ahead of them. Gradually 4th Armoured Brigade began to arrive, but so did Italian tanks. Despite several days of intense but disorganised attacks the Italians failed to break through and ultimately surrendered. It was an ignominious defeat and when it was over the reunited 11th Hussars, now joined by their replacements, the Kings Dragoon Guards equipped with Marmon-Herringtons, continued to scout the road up to the Tripolitanian frontier, making their temporary home in the captured Italian fort at El Agheila. Here they learned that what was left of the 7th Armoured Division, of which 11th Hussars were a part, were to be recalled to Cairo, where the regiment would finally dispose of its Rolls-Royces in exchange for more modern vehicles.

It remains to mention that No 2 Armoured Car Company, Royal Air Force, the erstwhile D Company in 11th Hussars, now transferred briefly to the Kings Dragoon Guards and joined them at El Agheila. Change was in the air and elements of the German Army, under General Erwin Rommel, had arrived, supported by the Luftwaffe, and it was these, replacing the Italians in the ground-attack role, that the armoured cars now encountered.

Mystery surrounds one particular picture, which shows Rolls-Royce armoured car 264 WO, knocked out and being inspected by Rommel. This car, now fitted with a Boys anti-tank rifle in the turret alongside the Vickers machine-gun, was one of the batch of six ordered by the RAF in March 1922, but what it was doing in the desert being inspected by General Rommel is not known.

According to the History of The Kings Dragoon Guards, although the RAF cars now passed under the control of that regiment it wasn't long – given the age of the few vehicles they had left and the time they had already spent in the North African desert – before they were summoned back to Cairo in the wake of the 11th Hussars, leaving the Kings Dragoon Guards feeling rather deserted and alone in a strange land.

Chapter Five

Anatomy of the Rolls-Royce armoured car

Most of this chapter is drawn from the Army's *1933 Instruction Book for the Rolls-Royce*. It describes the features and specifications of the car in the distinctive language of the period.

OPPOSITE The Tank Museum's Rolls-Royce 1920-pattern Mark I Armoured Car, chassis number 117WO. *(10155-032)*

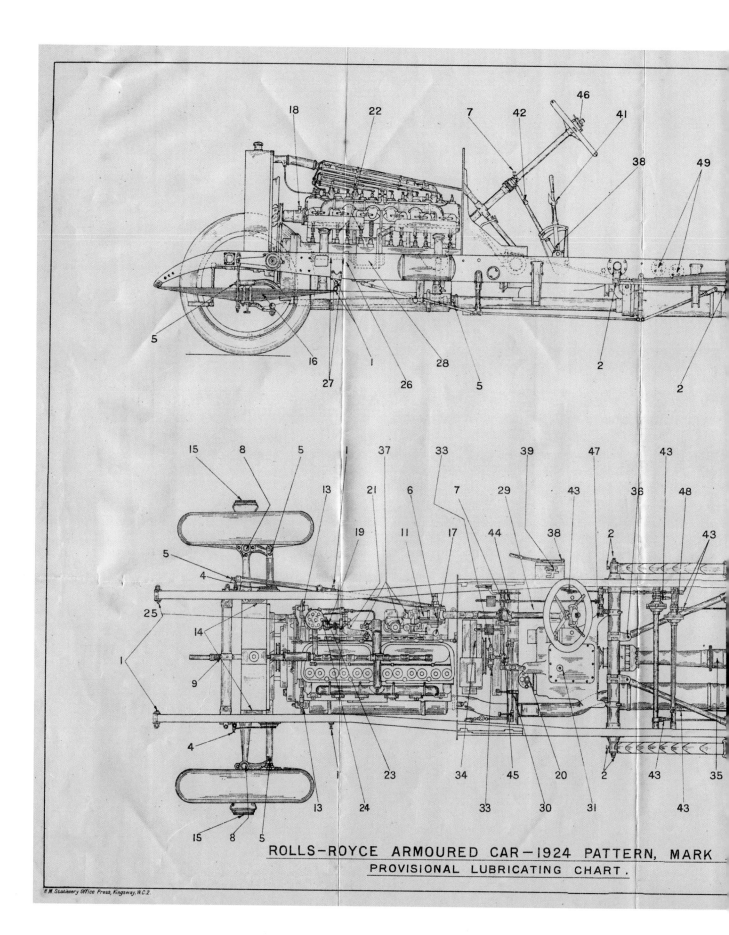

ROLLS-ROYCE ARMOURED CAR—1924 PATTERN, MARK
PROVISIONAL LUBRICATING CHART.

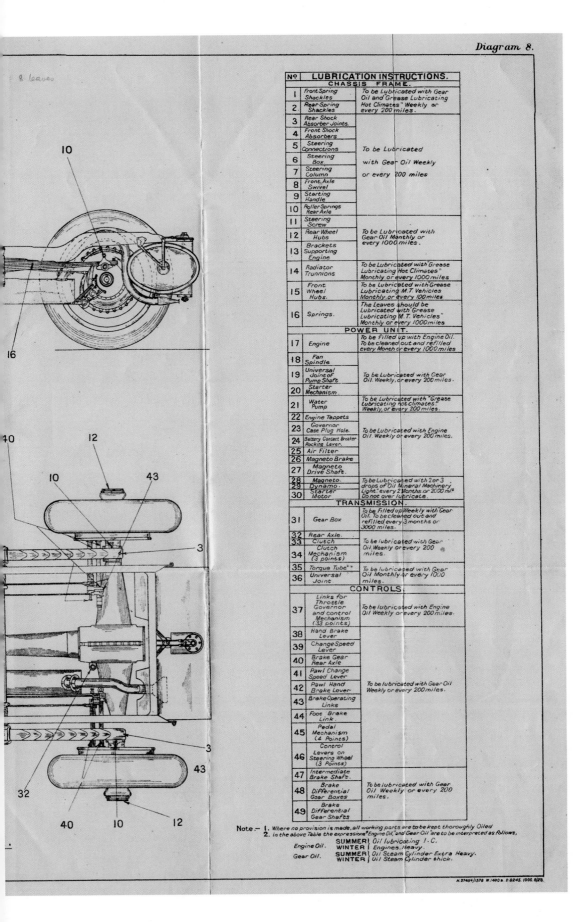

Diagram 8.

Nº		LUBRICATION INSTRUCTIONS.
		CHASSIS FRAME.
1	Front Spring Shackles	To be Lubricated with Gear Oil and "Grease Lubricating Hot Climates" Weekly or every 200 miles.
2	Rear Spring Shackles	
3	Rear Shock Absorber Joints.	
4	Front Shock Absorbers	To be Lubricated with Gear Oil Weekly or every 200 miles
5	Steering Connections	
6	Steering Box.	
7	Steering Column	
8	Front Axle Swivel	
9	Starting Handle	
10	Roller Springs Rear Axle	
11	Steering Screw	
12	Rear Wheel Hubs	To be Lubricated with Gear Oil Monthly or every 1000 miles.
13	Brackets Supporting Engine	
14	Radiator Trunnions	To be Lubricated with "Grease Lubricating Hot Climates" Monthly or every 1000 miles
15	Front Wheel Hubs.	To be Lubricated with "Grease Lubricating M.T. Vehicles" Monthly or every 1000 miles
16	Springs.	The Leaves should be Lubricated with "Grease Lubricating M.T. Vehicles" Monthly or every 1000 miles
		POWER UNIT.
17	Engine	To be Filled up with Engine Oil. To be cleaned out and refilled every Month or every 1000 miles
18	Fan Spindle	
19	Universal Joint of Pump Shaft	To be Lubricated with Gear Oil Weekly, or every 200 miles.
20	Starter Mechanism	
21	Water Pump	To be Lubricated with "Grease Lubricating hot climates". Weekly or every 200 miles.
22	Engine Tappets	
23	Governor Case Plug Hole.	To be Lubricated with Engine Oil Weekly or every 200 miles.
24	Battery Contact Breaker Rocking Lever.	
25	Air Filter	
26	Magneto Brake	
27	Magneto Drive Shaft.	
28	Magneto.	To be Lubricated with 2 or 3 drops of Oil "Mineral Machinery Light" every 2 Months or 2000 m/s. Do not over lubricate.
29	Dynamo.	
30	Starter Motor	
		TRANSMISSION.
31	Gear Box	To be Filled up Weekly with Gear Oil. To be cleaned out and refilled every 3 months or 3000 miles.
32	Rear Axle.	
33	Clutch	To be lubricated with Gear Oil Weekly or every 200 miles.
34	Clutch Mechanism (3 points)	
35	Torque Tube * *	To be lubricated with Gear Oil Monthly or every 1000 miles.
36	Universal Joint	
		CONTROLS.
37	Links for Throttle Governor and control Mechanism (33 points)	To be lubricated with Engine Oil Weekly or every 200 miles.
38	Hand Brake Lever	
39	Change Speed Lever	
40	Brake Gear Rear Axle	
41	Pawl Change Speed Lever	
42	Pawl Hand Brake Lever	To be lubricated with Gear Oil Weekly or every 200 miles.
43	Brake Operating Links	
44	Foot Brake Link.	
45	Pedal Mechanism (4 Points)	
46	Control Levers on Steering Wheel (3 Points)	
47	Intermediate Brake Shaft.	To be lubricated with Gear Oil Weekly or every 200 miles.
48	Brake Differential Gear Boxes	
49	Brake Differential Gear Shafts	

Note.— 1. Where no provision is made, all working parts are to be kept thoroughly Oiled
2. In the above Table the expressions "Engine Oil," and "Gear Oil" are to be interpreted as follows,
Engine Oil. { SUMMER| Oil lubricating I.C. / WINTER | Engines. Heavy.
Gear Oil. { SUMMER| Oil Steam Cylinder Extra Heavy. / WINTER | Oil Steam Cylinder thick.

8 leaves

LEFT Rolls-Royce Armoured Car 1924-pattern Mark I, lubrication chart, showing the construction of the chassis. *(E1949.24)*

RIGHT A Silver Ghost chassis at Vickers Ltd's Erith works, shortly to be completed as an armoured car for India.

Chassis

Before the Second World War Rolls-Royce only built the chassis for their cars. Private owners could choose their car's bodywork from a number of different coachbuilders. The same was true of the armoured cars.

This form of construction had an advantage in later years – as the old chassis wore out, the armoured bodies could be removed and fitted to new ones, which could come from any manufacturer.

Not only did this give the cars a new lease of life, but, importantly, it cost the Army less money than a full replacement vehicle would.

BELOW A Silver Ghost chassis in India. With the armoured body lifted off it was still possible to drive, although improvised wooden seats had to be fitted.

This was done with many 1914-pattern bodies between the wars.

The chassis consisted of two side girders braced by five cross members and the radiator. The 1920-pattern armoured car chassis differed from the civilian Silver Ghost as a sixth cross member was added to give greater strength at the rear axle. This was due to the stronger springs and double wheels that were necessary to support the extra weight of the armoured body. Civilian or military, the bare chassis was strong enough to be driven without a body fitted.

Bodywork

In common with other armoured fighting vehicles of this class, the armoured bodies of these cars include:

■ A body proper for accommodating the crew and driver
■ A revolving turret on which is mounted a hood
■ A forward portion which enclosed the engine compartment.

The armoured body proper constitutes the fighting chamber, which has a double-leaf door, secured from the inside, at the rear.

LEFT Right-side profile. *(10155-042)*

BELOW Left-side profile. *(10155-043)*

On the offside of the body adjacent to the driver's seat is an aperture for the driver's use for general observation and signalling. The driver's lookout is protected by an adjustable hinged flap of bulletproof steel having a lookout port for use when the flap is closed.

The turret, mounted above the body, is supported on steel rollers which enable it to be rotated freely on a circular path. These rollers can be raised clear of their path and, by employing a locking device, the turret is prevented from rotating when the vehicle is travelling or not in action.

At the forward end of the engine compartment double-leaf doors with louvres are fitted. These are operated by the driver, thus controlling the amount of cooling air which is admitted to the radiator and, when closed, affording complete protection to the radiator.

A bulletproof shield protects the underside of the engine compartment while bulletproof steel angle plates, arranged diagonally on the cover, serve to deflect machine-gun and rifle fire.

The exposed portion of the vehicle behind the body is utilised for the stowage of tools, spares and equipment, which are housed in lockers carried on platforms arranged as mudguards over the rear wheels.

Protective armour encloses the main petrol tank underslung at the rear of the vehicle.

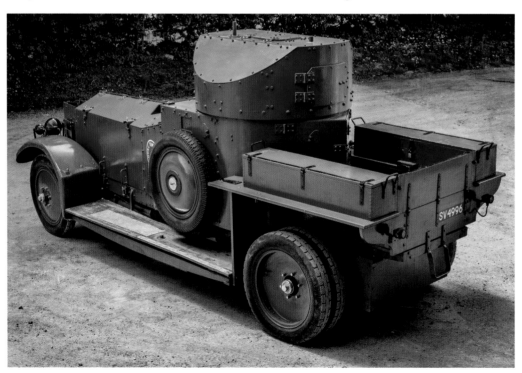

ABOVE The armoured radiator doors are opened . . . *(10155-021)*

LEFT . . . and closed by a lever on the dashboard. *(10155-020)*

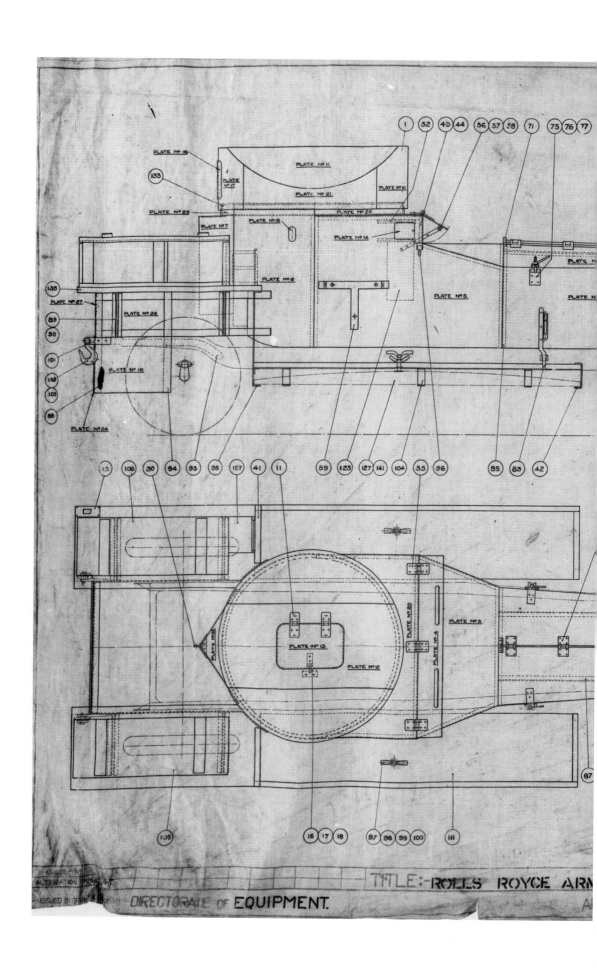

TITLE:-ROLLS ROYCE ARM

DIRECTORATE OF EQUIPMENT.

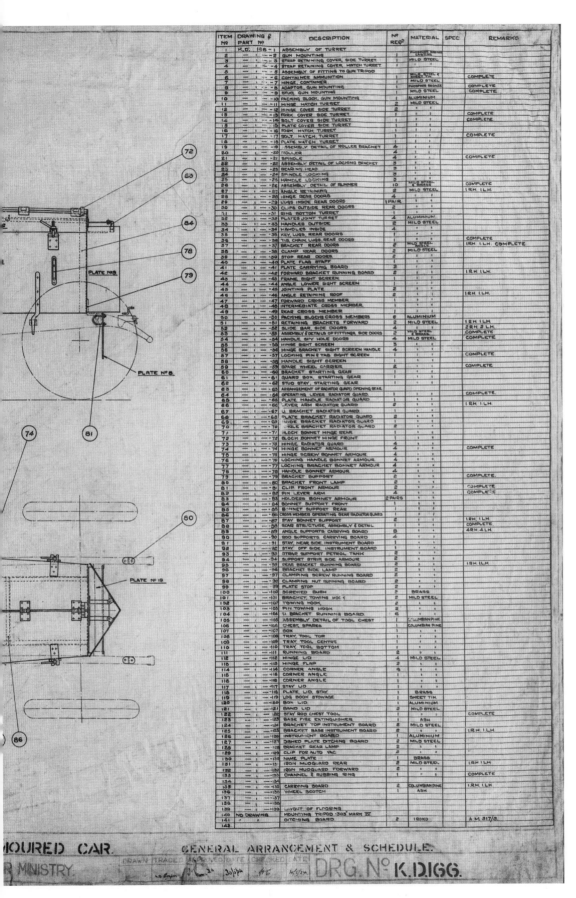

ITEM Nº	DRAWING & PART Nº	DESCRIPTION	Nº REQD	MATERIAL	SPEC	REMARKS
1	K.D. 166 - 1	ASSEMBLY OF TURRET				
2	„ „ - 2	GUN MOUNTING		DURALUMIN CASTING		
3	„ „ - 3	STRAP RETAINING COVER, SIDE TURRET	1	MILD STEEL		
4	„ „ - 4	STRAP RETAINING COVER, HATCH TURRET	1			
5	„ „ - 5	ASSEMBLY OF FITTING TO GUN TRIPOD		MILD STEEL &		
6	„ „ - 6	CONTAINER AMMUNITION		MILD STEEL		COMPLETE
7	„ „ - 7	HINGE, CONTAINER	1	PHOSPHOR BRONZE		
8	„ „ - 8	ADAPTOR, GUN MOUNTING		MILD STEEL		COMPLETE
9	„ „ - 9	STUD, GUN MOUNTING		MILD STEEL		COMPLETE
10	„ „ - 10	PACKING BLOCK, GUN MOUNTING		ALUMINIUM		
11	„ „ - 11	HINGE HATCH TURRET	2	MILD STEEL		
12	„ „ - 12	HINGE COVER SIDE TURRET	2	„ „		
13	„ „ - 13	FORK COVER SIDE TURRET	1	„ „		COMPLETE
14	„ „ - 14	BOLT COVER SIDE TURRET	1	„ „		COMPLETE
15	„ „ - 15	PLATE COVER SIDE TURRET	1	„ „		
16	„ „ - 16	FORK HATCH TURRET	1	„ „		
17	„ „ - 17	BOLT, HATCH, TURRET	1	„ „		COMPLETE
18	„ „ - 18	PLATE, HATCH, TURRET	1	„ „		
19	„ „ - 19	ASSEMBLY DETAIL OF ROLLER BRACKET	4	„ „		
20	„ „ - 20	ROLLER	4	„ „		
21	„ „ - 21	SPINDLE	4	„ „		COMPLETE
22	„ „ - 22	ASSEMBLY DETAIL OF LOCKING BRACKET	3	„ „		
23	„ „ - 23	BEARING HEAD	3	„ „		
24	„ „ - 24	SPINDLE LOCKING	3	„ „		
25	„ „ - 25	HANDLE LOCKING	3	„ „		
26	„ „ - 26	ASSEMBLY DETAIL OF RUNNER	10	MILD STEEL & BRASS		COMPLETE
27	„ „ - 27	ANGLE RETAINING	2	MILD STEEL		1 R.H. 1 L.H.
28	„ „ - 28	HINGE REAR DOORS	2	„ „		
29	„ „ - 29	LUGS INSIDE REAR DOORS	1 PAIR	„ „		
30	„ „ - 30	CLIPS OUTSIDE REAR DOORS	2	„ „		
31	„ „ - 31	RING BOTTOM TURRET	1	ALUMINIUM		
32	„ „ - 32	PLATES JOINT TURRET	4	MILD STEEL		
33	„ „ - 33	HANDLES OUTSIDE	2	„ „		
34	„ „ - 34	HANDLES INSIDE	4	„ „		
35	„ „ - 35	KEY LUGS, REAR DOORS	1	„ „		COMPLETE
36	„ „ - 36	TAB CHAIN, LUGS, REAR DOORS	1	„ „		1 R.H. 1 L.H. COMPLETE
37	„ „ - 37	BRACKET REAR DOORS	2	MILD STEEL		
38	„ „ - 38	CLAMP REAR DOORS	2	MILD STEEL		
39	„ „ - 39	STOP REAR DOORS	2	„ „		
40	„ „ - 40	PLATE FLAG STAFF	1	„ „		
41	„ „ - 41	PLATE CARRYING BOARD	2	„ „		
42	„ „ - 42	FORWARD BRACKET RUNNING BOARD	2	„ „		1 R.H. 1 L.H.
43	„ „ - 43	FRAME SIGHT SCREEN	1	„ „		
44	„ „ - 44	ANGLE LOWER SIGHT SCREEN	1	„ „		
45	„ „ - 45	JOINTING PLATE	2	„ „		
46	„ „ - 46	ANGLE RETAINING ROOF	2	„ „		1 R.H. 1 L.H.
47	„ „ - 47	FORWARD CROSS MEMBER	1	„ „		
48	„ „ - 48	INTERMEDIATE CROSS MEMBER	1	„ „		
49	„ „ - 49	REAR CROSS MEMBER	1	ALUMINIUM		
50	„ „ - 50	PACKING BLOCKS CROSS MEMBERS	6	MILD STEEL		1 R.H. 1 L.H.
51	„ „ - 51	RETAINING BRACKETS FORWARD	2	„ „		2 R.H. 2 L.H.
52	„ „ - 52	SLIDE BAR SIDE DOORS	2	MILD STEEL & BRASS		COMPLETE
53	„ „ - 53	ASSEMBLY & DETAILS OF FITTINGS, SIDE DOORS	2	MILD STEEL		COMPLETE
54	„ „ - 54	HANDLE, SPY HOLE DOORS	4	MILD STEEL		
55	„ „ - 55	HINGE SIGHT SCREEN	3	„ „		
56	„ „ - 56	HINGE BRACKET SIGHT SCREEN HANDLE	4	„ „		
57	„ „ - 57	LOCKING PIN & TAB SIGHT SCREEN	1	„ „		COMPLETE
58	„ „ - 58	HANDLE SIGHT SCREEN	1	„ „		
59	„ „ - 59	SPARE WHEEL CARRIER	2	„ „		COMPLETE
60	„ „ - 60	BRACKET STARTING GEAR	1	„ „		
61	„ „ - 61	GUARD BOX, STARTING GEAR	1	„ „		
62	„ „ - 62	STUD STAY, STARTING GEAR	1	„ „		
63	„ „ - 63	ARRANGEMENT OF RADIATOR GUARD OPENING GEAR		„ „		
64	„ „ - 64	OPERATING LEVER RADIATOR GUARD	1	„ „		COMPLETE.
65	„ „ - 65	PLATE, HANDLE, RADIATOR GUARD	1	„ „		
66	„ „ - 66	LEVER ARM RADIATOR GUARD	2	„ „		1 R.H. 1 L.H.
67	„ „ - 67	U BRACKET RADIATOR GUARD	1	„ „		
68	„ „ - 68	PLATE BRACKET RADIATOR GUARD	2	„ „		
69	„ „ - 69	INSIDE BRACKET RADIATOR GUARD	1	„ „		
70	„ „ - 70	ANGLE BRACKET RADIATOR GUARD	2	„ „		
71	„ „ - 71	BLOCK BONNET HINGE REAR	1	„ „		
72	„ „ - 72	BLOCK BONNET HINGE FRONT	1	„ „		
73	„ „ - 73	HINGE, RADIATOR GUARD	4	„ „		
74	„ „ - 74	HINGE BONNET ARMOUR	4	„ „		COMPLETE
75	„ „ - 75	HINGE SCREW BONNET ARMOUR	4	„ „		
76	„ „ - 76	LOCKING HANDLE BONNET ARMOUR	4	„ „		
77	„ „ - 77	LOCKING BRACKET BONNET ARMOUR	4	„ „		
78	„ „ - 78	HANDLE BONNET ARMOUR	4	„ „		
79	„ „ - 79	BRACKET SUPPORT	2	„ „		COMPLETE.
80	„ „ - 80	BRACKET FRONT LAMP	2	„ „		
81	„ „ - 81	CLIP FRONT ARMOUR	2	„ „		COMPLETE
82	„ „ - 82	PIN LEVER ARM	1	„ „		COMPLETE
83	„ „ - 83	HOLDERS BONNET ARMOUR	2 PAIRS	„ „		
84	„ „ - 84	BONNET SUPPORT FRONT	1	„ „		
85	„ „ - 85	BONNET SUPPORT REAR	1	„ „		
86	„ „ - 86	CROSS MEMBER OPERATING GEAR RADIATOR GUARD	1	„ „		L.H. 1 R.H.
87	„ „ - 87	STAY BONNET SUPPORT	2	„ „		COMPLETE.
88	„ „ - 88	REAR STRUCTURE, ASSEMBLY & DETAIL	1	„ „		4 R.H. 4 L.H.
89	„ „ - 89	ANGLE SUPPORTS CARRYING BOARD	8	„ „		
90	„ „ - 90	ROD SUPPORTS CARRYING BOARD	4	„ „		
91	„ „ - 91	STAY, NEAR SIDE, INSTRUMENT BOARD	1	„ „		
92	„ „ - 92	STAY, OFF SIDE, INSTRUMENT BOARD	1	„ „		
93	„ „ - 93	STRAP SUPPORT PETROL TANK	2	„ „		
94	„ „ - 94	SUPPORT STRIP SIDE ARMOUR	2	„ „		
95	„ „ - 95	REAR BRACKET RUNNING BOARD	2	„ „		1 R.H. 1 L.H.
96	„ „ - 96	BRACKET SIDE LAMP	2	„ „		
97	„ „ - 97	CLAMPING SCREW RUNNING BOARD	2	„ „		
98	„ „ - 98	CLAMPING NUT RUNNING BOARD	2	„ „		
99	„ „ - 99	PLATE STOP	2	„ „		
100	„ „ - 100	SCREWED BUSH	2	BRASS		
101	„ „ - 101	BRACKET, TOWING HOOK	2	MILD STEEL		
102	„ „ - 102	TOWING HOOK	1	„ „		
103	„ „ - 103	PIN TOWING HOOK	2	„ „		
104	„ „ - 104	U BRACKET RUNNING BOARD	6	„ „		
105	„ „ - 105	ASSEMBLY DETAIL OF TOOL CHEST		COLUMBIAN PINE		
106	„ „ - 106	CHEST, SPARES		COLUMBIAN PINE		
107	„ „ - 107	BOX				
108	„ „ - 108	TRAY, TOOL TOP				
109	„ „ - 109	TRAY, TOOL CENTRE				
110	„ „ - 110	TRAY, TOOL BOTTOM				
111	„ „ - 111	RUNNING BOARD	2			
112	„ „ - 112	HINGE LID	4	MILD STEEL		
113	„ „ - 113	HINGE FLAP	2	„ „		
114	„ „ - 114	CORNER ANGLE	8	„ „		
115	„ „ - 115	CORNER ANGLE	1	„ „		
116	„ „ - 116	CORNER ANGLE	1	„ „		
117	„ „ - 117	STAY LID	1	„ „		
118	„ „ - 118	PLATE, LID, STAY	1	BRASS		
119	„ „ - 119	LOG BOOK STOWAGE	1	SHEET TIN		
120	„ „ - 120	BOX LID	1	ALUMINIUM		
121	„ „ - 121	BAND LID	2	MILD STEEL		
122	„ „ - 122	STAY ROD CHEST TOOL	1	„ „		COMPLETE
123	„ „ - 123	BASE FIRE EXTINGUISHER	1	ASH		
124	„ „ - 124	BRACKET TOP INSTRUMENT BOARD	2	MILD STEEL		
125	„ „ - 125	BRACKET BASE INSTRUMENT BOARD	2	„ „		1 R.H. 1 L.H.
126	„ „ - 126	INSTRUMENT BOARD	1	ALUMINIUM		
127	„ „ - 127	DISHED PLATE DITCHING BOARD	2	MILD STEEL		
128	„ „ - 128	BRACKET REAR LAMP	2	„ „		
129	„ „ - 129	CLIP FOR AUTO VAC	1	„ „		
130	„ „ - 130	NAME PLATE	1	BRASS		
131	„ „ - 131	IRON MUDGUARD REAR	2	MILD STEEL		1 R.H. 1 L.H.
132	„ „ - 132	IRON MUDGUARD FORWARD	2	„ „		
133	„ „ - 133	CHANNEL & RUBBING RING	1	„ „		COMPLETE
134	„ „ - 134					
135	„ „ - 135	CARRYING BOARD	2	COLUMBIAN PINE		1 R.H. 1 L.H.
136	„ „ - 136	WHEEL SCOTCH	1	ASH		
137	„ „ - 137					
138	„ „ - 138					
139	„ „ - 139	LAYOUT OF FLOORING				
140	NO DRAWING	MOUNTING TRIPOD ·303· MARK IV	2			A.M. 317/3.
141	„ „	DITCHING BOARD		IRON WOOD		
142						

MOURED CAR. | **GENERAL ARRANGEMENT & SCHEDULE.**

R MINISTRY.

DRAWN | TRACED | APPROVED | DATE | CHECKED | DATE | **DRG. Nº K.D166.**

Suspension

Front springs

The front springs are semi-elliptic. The front end is anchored by means of a pin bearing to a bush in the dumb iron, while at the rear end a short shackle is employed to connect it to the frame.

Rear springs

The rear springs are full cantilever, bearing at their centres on swivel pins bolted to the frame by brackets. The swivel pins pass underneath the frame and are anchored at their inner ends to a cross member. The front end of each spring is secured to the chassis frame by means of a shackle and the rear end rests on a flanged roller on the back axle casing.

Steering

General description

The steering gear, contained in the steering box, is of the worm and nut type, cut with a right-handed, three-start thread, the worm being on the central column, while the nut works in a plain bearing on the rocking shaft which is mounted in two ball races. The nut is of phosphor bronze made in two halves, for assembling purposes, and bolted together. To allow the nut

to describe an arc in its travel, vertical movement is given to the central column, which pivots in a thrust bearing halfway between the steering box and the steering wheel.

Actuation

The movement of the rocking shaft is conveyed through the drop arm, which is splined to it, to the side steering tube, spring loaded at each end to absorb the shock, and thence to the steering lever bolted to the top of the offside pivot axle. Bolted to the bottom of the offside pivot axle is a cross steering lever, which carries the movement through the cross steering tube to a similar lever on the near side pivot axle.

Brakes

Handbrake

The handbrake is of the internal expanding type and works on a drum in the rear hub. There are two brake shoes lined with cast iron which are operated by an 'S'-shaped cam. The hand lever is on the right side of the driver and is connected to the brake levers through the brake compensating mechanism by cables.

The compensating mechanism consists of a small differential gear and ensures that the brakes are applied to both wheels with equal pressures.

Footbrake

The footbrake is of the internal expanding type and works on the larger of the two drums in the rear hub. There are two brake shoes, lined with Ferodo, and operated by an 'S'-shaped cam. The footbrake pedal is just to the right of the steering column and is connected to the brake levers through the compensating mechanism by cables. The compensating mechanism is similar to that used on the handbrake. Fitted on the offside of the chassis is a milled head nut for quick adjustment.

Wheels and tyres

The first armoured cars had triple-spoked wire wheels, which were standard on the civilian car from 1913. They were usually manufactured by Dunlop or Rudge-Whitworth. Unlike civilian cars, the rear axle was fitted with twin wheels to support the extra weight.

Some early cars had solid rubber tyres,

but most used pneumatic ones, which were vulnerable under fire and in the difficult terrain of India and the desert. The 1920-pattern cars replaced these with Michelin steel disc wheels and 895 × 150mm Palmer cord tyres.

In India the cars were fitted with narrow steel disc wheels and Macintosh normal air pressure (NAP) tyres. NAPs were solid rubber with triangular air pockets on the circumference which gave an element of cushioning. They could slip and skid in bad conditions, but they stood up far better than pneumatic tyres to the harsh conditions of the Indian environment.

During their final years, the Rolls-Royces were often fitted with split-rim wheels and large-section tyres, especially in the desert.

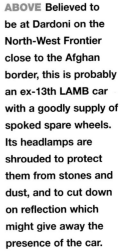

ABOVE Believed to be at Dardoni on the North-West Frontier close to the Afghan border, this is probably an ex-13th LAMB car with a goodly supply of spoked spare wheels. Its headlamps are shrouded to protect them from stones and dust, and to cut down on reflection which might give away the presence of the car.

LEFT A 7th ACC car photographed near Razmak. Clearly shown are the disc wheels and Macintosh NAP tyres, although a spare is unusual. Notice also the rifle loopholes in the turret.

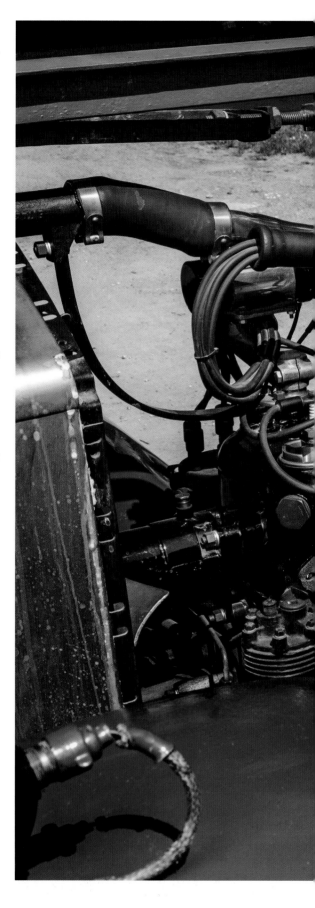

Engine

Description

■ 40/50hp Rolls-Royce, six-cylinder, water-cooled engine

■ Bore 4.5in, stroke 4.75in, max 82bhp at 2,250rpm

■ Weight 996lb.

Cylinders

The cylinders are cast in two blocks of three cylinders each. They are of the inverted L-type and are water jacketed.

Valves

The valves, which are side by side, are of specially toughened stainless steel, concave and streamlined and are interchangeable. They are actuated by a camshaft through rocker arms fitted with rollers which bear upon the cams. The tappets, working in hardened steel guides, are fitted with springs to ensure a constant bearing between cams, rollers and tappets. The rocker gear is lubricated by splash and each rocker is contained in a detachable cast aluminium cover. One spiral coil spring is fitted to each valve. Both inlet and exhaust valve guides are water cooled and fitted with removable bronze liners.

Pistons

Aluminium alloy cast, with convex top and split skirt. They are fitted with six rings, the top ring being free to revolve and the other five pegged. The hollow gudgeon pin is secured by a locking screw at each end. These screws pass upwards through the gudgeon pin housing, inside the skirt and are threaded into the gudgeon pin. They are prevented from revolving by split pins.

Connecting rods

'H'-section high-tensile steel forging with floating bronze bush at the small end and white metal bearing at the big end. A small copper pipe for lubrication runs from the big end to the small end.

Crankshaft

Machined all over from chrome nickel steel forging drilled throughout for lubrication. Six throw, running in seven gunmetal bearings, white metal lined.

Flywheel

Bolted to a flange on the rear end of the crankshaft. A ring bolted to the rear face of the flywheel forms the outer member of the clutch and is fitted with a plug for draining any excess oil in the clutch.

Vibration damper

Keyed on the front end of the crankshaft is a flange on each side of which there is a friction flywheel of larger diameter. These flywheels grip the flange between them by means of 20 spring bolts which pass through their outer circumference. Between each of the flywheels and the flange there is a fibre washer. The vibration damper is contained in the timing pinion case.

Camshaft

Of case hardened nickel chrome steel running in seven phosphor bronze bearings. The camshaft is driven by helical gearing direct from the main timing pinion.

Timing gears

The timing pinions are helical toothed. The main timing pinion is of steel and is spring driven from the crankshaft. On the right side of this is the intermediate pinion of phosphor bronze which drives the steel water pump pinion. The water pump shaft drives, by worm gearing, a vertical shaft which operates the battery distributor and contact breaker, the air pump, the governor and the oil pump. In mesh with the main timing pinion on the left is the camshaft pinion, of phosphor bronze, and, driven from this, is the steel magneto pinion.

Transmission

Clutch

The clutch used is an internal cone clutch lined with cotton fabric, fastened to the inner cone with copper wire. The fabric is lubricated by oil being squirted on to the fabric when necessary, and the oil is prevented from escaping by an oil-retaining ring bolted to the flywheel.

The spigot end bearing is lubricated by oil from the hollow crankshaft. This is controlled by a valve fitted in the spigot end. When the clutch pedal is depressed, a plunger opens the valve and allows a small quantity of oil to escape from the crankshaft into the bearing.

The clutch stop consists of a ring bolted to the inner cone, which upon the clutch being depressed is brought into contact with a fibre pad fitted on a spring lever.

Gearbox

The gearbox gives four forward speeds and one reverse at the following ratios, using back axle reductions of:

	16/52	14/52
1st gear	11.07	12.65
2nd gear	7.22	8.25
3rd gear	4.86	5.52
4th gear	3.25	3.71
Reverse	11.07	12.65

It is divided into three compartments. The forward compartment contains the constant mesh

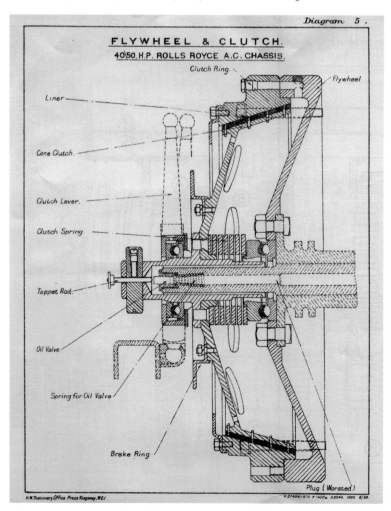

Diagram 5.

FLYWHEEL & CLUTCH.
40\50.H.P. ROLLS ROYCE A.C. CHASSIS.

Clutch Ring
Flywheel
Liner
Cone Clutch.
Clutch Lever.
Clutch Spring
Tappet Rod.
Oil Valve.
Spring for Oil Valve
Brake Ring
Plug (Worsted.)

H.M.Stationery Office Press Kingsway,W.C.I

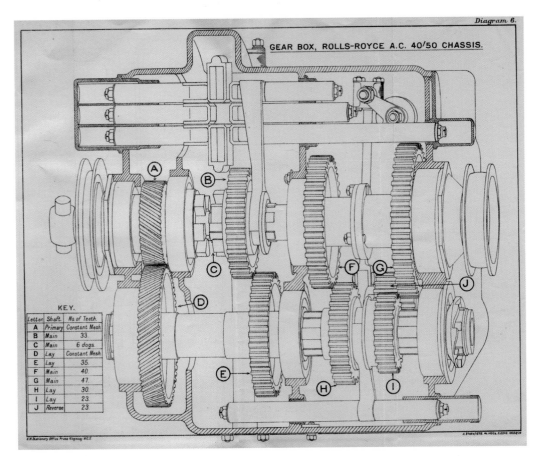

Diagram 6.

GEAR BOX, ROLLS-ROYCE A.C. 40/50 CHASSIS.

KEY.

Letter	Shaft	No. of Teeth.
A	Primary	Constant Mesh.
B	Main	33.
C	Main	6 dogs.
D	Lay	Constant Mesh.
E	Lay	35.
F	Main	40.
G	Main	47.
H	Lay	30.
I	Lay	23.
J	Reverse	23.

pinions, which are helical toothed. The middle compartment carries the pinions for giving 3rd and 4th speeds and 1st and 2nd speed pinions are found in the rear compartment.

The primary shaft is carried in two ball-bearings and the main and lay shafts each in three bearings, the front bearing of the main shaft in the primary shaft being a plain bearing and all the others ball-bearings.

The splined pinions for obtaining 1st and 2nd speeds are on the lay shaft and that for 3rd moves on the main shaft; 4th speed is obtained by dogs on the forward side of the 3rd speed pinion engaging in dogs on the end of the primary shaft.

A broad pinion, mounted on a bush on an excentric fitted in the bottom of the gearbox, provides reverse gear by meshing between the 1st speed pinions on the main and lay shafts.

In addition to a safety device in the gearbox to prevent any two gears from engaging at the same time, the gear lever is spring loaded and the gate fitted with retaining notches so that there can be no possibility of slipping out of gear.

The starter motor mechanism is fitted to the gearbox and is driven by chain and sprocket by the starter motor. The drive incorporates a small safety clutch and after three successive reductions (by two epicyclics and a chain reduction) is carried by a splined tube passing through the hollow lay shaft to a sliding jaw clutch fitted outside a similar clutch splined to the rear end of the lay shaft.

When the self-starter push button switch is pressed, the sliding or rear half of this clutch is drawn forward by means of an electric magnet and is engaged with the fixed portion, this allowing the starter motor to revolve the lay shaft and to start the engine. The total gear reduction between the motor starter and the engine is 23.33 to 1.

To replenish the oil in the gearbox the cover should be removed.

The correct level of oil in the gearbox is 5.75in from the cover joint. A plug is fitted to each of the centre and rear compartments for draining.

The differential

This is of the spur tooth type and contains four pairs of planetary pinions. The cage is supported by two ball races and embodied in it

RIGHT The notebook
of Private J. Dodds of
the 2nd ACC, Royal
Tank Corps. In August
1924 Dodds was
instructed on the use
of the Rolls-Royce
armoured car and
like many soldiers,
before and after, he
wrote up his notes
with helpful diagrams.
This one shows
the arrangement
of the differential.
(E2010.3966.003)

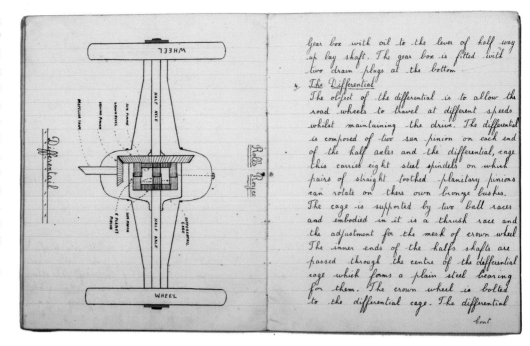

is a thrust race and adjustment for the mesh of the crown wheel. The crown wheel is driven by a bevel pinion.

The whole is surrounded by the rear axle casing to which the torque tube is bolted.

The differential is lubricated by oil which should be kept to the level of the filler plug on the near side of the casing.

Shafts and couplings

The clutch coupling is of the sliding sleeve type fitted over blocks and trunnions on the inner member of the clutch and the primary shaft of the gearbox. The coupling is lubricated through an oil hole at the rear end of the sleeve.

Connecting the main shaft of the gearbox with the propeller shaft is a ring-type universal joint. The tubular connection with its outer ring is bolted to a flange on the main shaft and its inner ring fits over the end of the propeller shaft and is splined. This joint is lubricated through a hole covered by a cap on the offside.

The propeller shaft is made in two halves with a splined ball joint in the middle. The front half is supported in its joint at each end and the rear half is supported in the torque tube by two ball-bearings, one just behind the splined coupling and one at the bevel pinion. The forward ball-bearing is lubricated through a cap-covered oil hole in the rear of the joint halfway down the torque tube.

The bevel pinion is keyed to the tapered end of the propeller shaft and further secured with locking nuts.

To take the driving thrust there is a thrust ball-bearing on the propeller shaft, just forward of the bevel pinion. This is lubricated from the rear axle casing.

The rear axles are of the full floating type, *ie*, the wheels being mounted on tubular continuations of the axle casing; the axle is subject to torsional stress only. Each half shaft is supported inside the cage on plain steel bearings. The outer end of the half shaft is splined and fits into the coupling drive which connects it to the inside of the hub by means of internal and external splines. There is no other support for the outer end of the half shaft.

Bolted to the front end of the torque tube is a hollow bronze ball made in two parts. This, by being bolted over a hollow steel ball held rigidly to the cross member immediately behind the gearbox, forms a flexible anchorage for the torque tube.

Petrol system

Carburettor

The four main portions that comprise the Rolls-Royce carburettor are the float chamber, the mixing chamber, the dashpot and the throttle.

The float actuates the needle valve, which is placed to the rear of it by means of a single lever at the bottom of the float chamber. The float chamber is fitted with a platform carrying two jets, each jet projecting into a separate vertical passage or choke tube. The amount of petrol drawn from the jets is controlled by a tapered valve fitted in the mouth of each jet. These valves can be raised or lowered from the steering column, thus giving a strong or weak mixture. The petrol is maintained at $\frac{1}{16}$in below the top of the jets. The airflow to the forward or low-speed jet is drawn from round the exhaust manifold through a pipe leading between the cylinder blocks. It enters the carburettor at the base of the jet, is drawn through the hot water jacketed choke tube into a small mixing chamber and thence through the water-heated barrel throttle into the induction pipe.

This jet gives a strong mixture for starting and slow running and is the only jet in operation until the engine exceeds about 750rpm.

Above the high-speed jet is fitted a dashpot consisting of a barrel and piston. From the piston is hung a disc which in its lowest position completely closes the high-speed choke tube. The suction of the engine draws air from the dashpot and, at speeds above 750rpm, causes the piston and valve to lift, thus opening the choke tube and allowing air to be drawn through the aluminium cowl fitted at the rear of the carburettor, past the high-speed jet into the high-speed mixing chamber. At still higher speeds, the dashpot piston is further lifted and uncovers slots cut in the base of the dashpot, admitting extra air direct to the mixing chamber.

BELOW Sectional drawing of the Smith five-jet carburettor from the Royal Tank Corps, India, lecture notes. *(E2010.3970.006)*

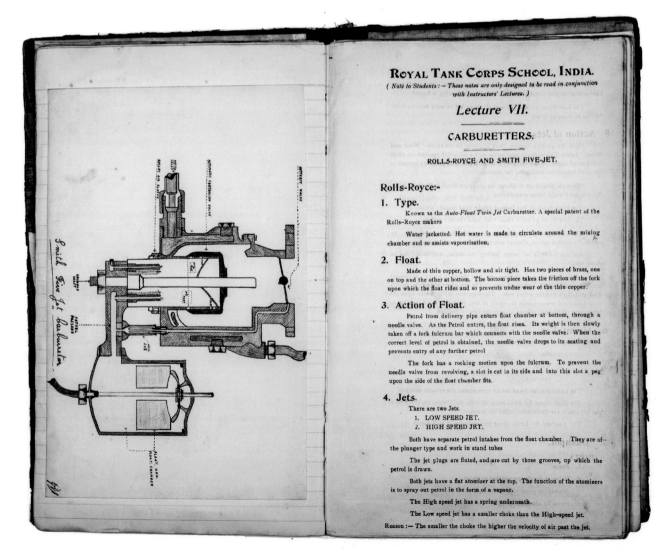

ABOVE
The carburettor.
(10155-003)

ABOVE RIGHT **The steering wheel with carburettor controls.**

Throttle and governor

The throttle is of the barrel type and is surrounded by a water jacket. It is so designed that should 'popping back' occur, it is closed automatically, thus preventing any possibility of fire.

The control of the throttle from the steering column is through the medium of the governor. The governor is connected with the throttle by means of rods and levers and its action is to close the throttle as engine speed is increased. Opposed to this action is a spring, the tension of which can be regulated by the governor lever on the steering column. The greater the tension that is put upon this spring, the faster must the engine revolve before the governor has sufficient power to close the throttle against this tension. The result of this mechanism is that when the governor lever is set, a constant road speed is maintained. The governor is prevented from coming into action when the accelerator is in use.

Petrol feed

The main petrol tank is situated at the rear of the car and contains 18 gallons. A cylindrical filter reaching to 0.75in from the bottom of the tank strains the petrol through a fine gauze as it is poured in. The petrol pipe is led from a separate partition in the base of the filter and through this the petrol is again strained as it leaves the tank. The feed to the carburettor is by pressure, produced by a hand pump fitted on the right side of the instrument board and maintained by the power pump driven by an excentric on the vertical shaft. The power pump can be regulated to maintain the correct pressure of 2lb psi by a milled screw found under a hexagonal cover on the forward end of the pump.

A four-way cock fitted on the chassis frame on the near side of the car directs the air pressure to the tank from either pump, separately, or from both pumps, according to the position in which it is set. It also enables the pressure to be released.

Priming device

A priming pipe is led from a junction in the hand pump pipe to the top of the induction manifold. It passes underneath the float chamber and is connected with it by a one-way valve, ensuring that the portion of the pipe lying below the petrol level is always filled with petrol. At its junction with the hand pump pipe there is a tap, which, in the priming position, directs the air pressure from the hand pump into the priming pipe, forcing the petrol that it contains

RIGHT **The four-way cock.** *(10155-010)*

into the induction manifold with each stroke of the hand pump.

When the tap is in the running position, it closes the connection between the hand pump and the priming pipe; it also closes the latter at its junction with the induction manifold, thus preventing petrol from being drawn from the priming pipe when the engine is running.

The priming tap is situated on the left side of the dashboard.

Auxiliary tank

An auxiliary petrol tank holding 5 gallons is placed between the instrument board and the dashboard. It is filled through a filler hole fitted with a cylindrical gauze filter and accessible through a sliding shutter in the front armour. A petrol pipe is led from the bottom of this tank and joins the main petrol pipe on the forward side of the dashboard. At this junction is fitted a tap by which the petrol may be turned off from both tanks or fed to the carburettor from either the main or auxiliary tank.

The tap is operated by a lever on the back of the auxiliary tank, under the right side of the instrument board.

The feed from the auxiliary tank is by gravity.

Ignition

General description

The car is fitted with dual ignition by a Watford magneto and the Rolls-Royce battery ignition set. There are two sparking plugs in each cylinder, one in the centre of the combustion chamber for the magneto ignition, and one in the inlet valve cap for the battery ignition.

The low-tension current for the battery ignition is produced from a 12-volt, 72-ampere/hour, accumulator which also provides the current for lighting and starting. There is a ballast resistance in the primary circuit to prevent damage to the coil.

The coil is placed on a bracket above the offside of the engine and the high-tension current is led from there to the centre terminal of the distributor rotor, which is driven by the vertical shaft.

The make and break, situated above the governor casing, is operated by a six-point cam on the vertical shaft.

Lubrication

General description

The lubrication of the engine is by the pressure system, assisted by oil mist. Oil is drawn from the sump, through a filter, by a gear-type pump and is forced to the main delivery pipe. From this there are six branch pipes. Three of these lead to the front, centre and rear main bearings, and then through the hollow crankshaft to the big ends. Oil is fed, under pressure, from the big end bearings through tubes attached to the connecting rods to the small ends. The oil escaping from each side of

ABOVE **The distributor.** *(10155-016)*

the big end bearing lubricates the walls of the cylinders and the camshaft bearings by oil mist.

Oil is delivered from the front branch pipe of the main delivery pipe to the timing gears. For automatically lubricating the cylinder walls at high speeds the fifth branch pipe is led to a valve controlled directly by the accelerator. When this is pressed down about two-thirds of its travel, the valve is opened and the oil is forced through small pipes to the cylinder walls. A sixth branch pipe leads to the oil gauge. There is a radial hole drilled through the crankshaft to feed the bush of the main timing pinion. An oil valve is fitted in the spigot end of the crankshaft to provide lubrication for the spigot end bush in the clutch hub.

The oil pump is fitted with an adjustable valve to regulate the oil pressure, which should show 15–20lb on the gauge. It is driven from the base of the vertical shaft by a square steel tube which acts as a safety device, spreading if the pump should jam.

The sump holds 1 gallon and is filled through a breather on the offside of the car. It can also be filled directly from a compartment of the auxiliary petrol tank holding 13 pints of oil. Sump oil level can be tested by a tap on the left side of the chassis.

Cooling

General description

The engine cooling is by pump circulation, a 3in centrifugal pump being used. The radiator is of the honeycomb type and a 22in fan with an excentric fan belt adjustment is fitted. The cooling system holds 9 gallons of water and can be drained by a cock underneath the pump. The pump drive is through a fibre universal joint connected with the spindle by a collar, which can slip on the spindle should the pump become jammed.

Electrics – lighting and starting

Lucas dynamo

Type E 575 – 12 volts. Current output of 12 amps at 12 volts at about 30mph. The field winding is shunt wound. The control brush is fitted on a moveable bracket between the positive and negative brushes. It can be moved through 15 degrees round the commutator. Current output is decreased by moving the control brush towards the negative brush (against the direction of rotation) and vice versa. The dynamo is mounted on a shaft which allows for lateral movement, the adjustment being on the side of the chassis.

BELOW Lubrication chart, 1928. *(E2012.2002)*

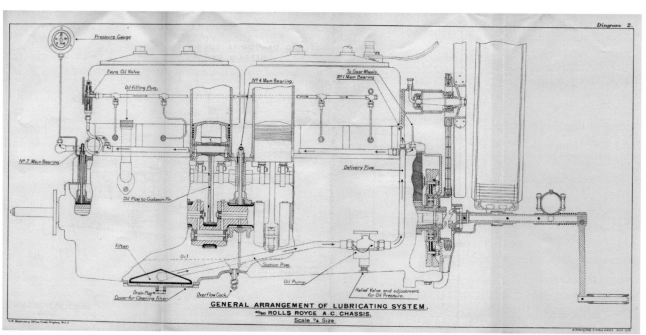

Starter motor

Rolls-Royce pattern. It is a series-wound four-pole motor. This ensures a powerful starting torque. The armature is wave wound and the conductors are series-connected. Four brushes set at 90 degrees are used. The normal current used for the initial start is 112 amps at 12 volts.

Switchboard

A Lucas-pattern switchboard is used and is suitable for controlling current up to 20 amps. It comprises:

- Magnetic cut-out in the charging circuit
- A fuse to protect the field winding of the dynamo
- A charging switch
- A switch for headlights
- A switch for sidelights
- Nine terminals
- Inspection lamp plugs.

Independent switches for tail and offside headlamps are also provided.

Ammeter

A Weston ammeter is fitted but is not incorporated in the switchboard. It is of the central zero type and registers up to 20 amps (charge or discharge).

Accumulator

A 12-volt, 72-ampere/hour battery is fitted. The containers are of moulded material and the plate separators are of specially prepared wood. When charging the battery from an external source, the charging rate should not exceed 8 amps, or the plates will be damaged by overheating.

Lamps

Two 24-watt headlamps; two 6-watt sidelamps, and a 6-watt tail lamp are fitted. These lamps are all controlled by the switches on the switchboard.

In addition, a separate switch operates the tail lamp independently. Two festoon lamps, with switch incorporated, are fitted to the instrument board. An electric klaxon horn is bolted to the front of the dashboard.

Weponry

The Rolls-Royce armoured car carried a number of weapons in its service career – the Maxim machine-gun, the Vickers machine-gun, the Lewis gun and, at the end of its service life, the Boys anti-tank rifle.

The cars' service was so widespread and lengthy that inevitably experiments were carried out with other armaments to meet local requirements. Crews would carry their own personal weapons – a variety can be seen in the images throughout this book – and accompanying troops were sometimes carried in the rear of the vehicle, so their weapons are also present.

Maxim and Vickers

The Vickers machine-gun begins with another famous name in the automatic weapon story – Hiram Maxim. Maxim, an American by birth, had invented and patented a filament-making process for electric lights. Thomas Edison and his associates were keen to clear the field of any rivals in the new electric light industry so they paid Maxim $20,000 a year to leave the USA and not pursue any further electric inventions for ten years. Maxim found his way to London in 1883 and turned his attention to developing guns. With support from the Vickers brothers he established the Maxim Gun Company in 1884 and displayed his very effective new machine-gun in a number of publicity stunts. Maxim saw a rival – though less impressive – product produced by the

ABOVE LEFT One of a pair of 24-watt headlamps.

ABOVE The single 6-watt tail lamp.

RIGHT **Hiram Maxim.**

RIGHT **The Vickers mounting from inside the turret.** *(10151-062)*

Nordenfelt Company, so merged his company and Nordenfelt together. In 1897 they were acquired by Vickers to create Vickers Sons & Maxim Ltd.

Maxim guns were used by the British military in a number of colonial wars – to great public acclaim. Partly as a result of their success, Maxim was knighted in 1901 and though remaining a paid director, retired from active work in the company. A number of improvements were made to his gun – the biggest being in 1907–8 when a new 'Light pattern' gun – now called the Vickers – emerged. It was just over half the weight of the original Maxim and was trialled and tested by the military. With small adjustments and improvements it was accepted by the War Office in November 1912 and so began over 50 years' service with the British Army. At the outbreak of the First World War there were 1,846 Maxims in British service, along with 109 Vickers. The great reliability of the Vickers saw it adopted by 30 other countries. It had an adjustable rate of fire that was between 450 and 600 rounds per minute. In a ground-mounted role the gun could be expected to fire up to 10,000 rounds an hour; a change of barrel would be required once an hour.

Lewis gun

The Lewis gun was also designed by an American, Isaac Newton Lewis – a colonel in the US Army. He worked up designs from earlier provided by Samuel Maclean but failed to sell the gun to the US military. Disappointed, Lewis retired from Army service and moved to Belgium to set up a company in Liège to manufacture the gun. The Birmingham Small Arms Company helped him iron out manufacturing difficulties and bought a licence from Lewis to start manufacturing the guns in England. Lewis closed and moved his factory to England just before the First World War and he became very rich from the royalty payments on the gun. The British Army adopted the gun in October 1915 and by the end of the First World War over 50,000 guns had been made in Britain and the USA. The gun was gas operated – with the distinctive shroud containing a fan of aluminium vanes to cool the barrel. The round pan magazines were available in two sizes –

FAR LEFT The Vickers .303 machine-gun with the smooth jacket. Production of a smooth water jacket began in late 1917 as it was quicker and cheaper to make than the fluted version. The tripod for the machine-gun was carried in the rear of the armoured car.

LEFT The Vickers .303 machine-gun on the ground tripod. This example carries the small tripod fixed to the water jacket, something that would not have been fitted in the armoured car as it would stop the easy removal of the gun from the turret mounting.

housing either 47 or 97 rounds. The rate of fire was 500–600 rounds per minute and versions of the gun were made for aircraft use without the distinctive cooling shroud. In the Second World War, especially in the early years when weapons were in short supply, some of these aircraft guns were fitted to vehicles.

Boys anti-tank rifle

The Germans were the first to introduce a dedicated anti-tank rifle – the T Gewehr – with a 13.2mm calibre in 1918. Despite its relative ineffectiveness – it was estimated in a test that none of the 18 rounds fired at a captured British Mark IV tank would have disabled it – many countries copied the idea. In the interwar period guns with a large-calibre armour-piercing bullet and a substantial charge of propellant were put into production in Finland, Switzerland, Poland, Russia, Germany and Britain.

The British design originated with Captain H.C. Boys, the Assistant Superintendent of Design at the Royal Small Arms Factory, Enfield. Boys died shortly before the gun was accepted for use in 1937 by the British Army. The name was changed from its original name – Stanchion – to Boys as a mark of respect.

The gun was a bolt-action rifle that had a five-shot magazine and fired .55in (or 13.9mm) rounds. The gun had a fierce recoil and despite being fitted with a muzzle brake, a slide for the barrel, a shock absorber on the front bipod and a rubber butt pad, firing the gun could still lead to bruising. The early ammunition could penetrate 23.2mm of armour plate at about 100yd – enough to go through a half track

and the lighter German tanks' frontal armour. However, with up-armouring and better-protected tanks, the Boys eventually lost its potency.

The role of the anti-tank rifle was taken over by hollow-charge weapons such as the bazooka, the PIAT and the Panzerfaust, but it retained its use in some armies as a high-powered sniping rifle.

BELOW The Lewis gun was replaced by the Bren gun as the Army's standard light machine-gun before the Second World War, but losses of material in France in 1940 meant older weapons were pressed back into service. The RAF and Royal Navy still had Lewis guns in use in a number of roles and their availability meant this type was fitted to a number of vehicles – including the Rolls-Royce armoured car.

BOTTOM The Boys anti-tank rifle fired a .55in projectile from a 5-round magazine that could penetrate up to 23mm of armour at 100yd. It was a big gun at over 5ft long and 35lb in weight, and gave a tremendous kick to the firer.

'You need to be confident driving in modern-day traffic at a possible 45mph, you certainly get the feeling it will do much more. Keep in mind this is a 96-year-old car that requires respect.'

Steve Latham, Tank Museum volunteer and Rolls-Royce driver

Chapter Six

Driving and maintenance: operating the Rolls-Royce armoured car

Ian Hudson and Steve Latham

Although it was based on a civilian vehicle and has many similar features to a modern car, there are some significant differences in how the Rolls-Royce armoured car is operated and maintained. Over the years, Tank Museum staff have learned the most effective ways to operate the vehicle, balancing our desire to demonstrate it with the need to preserve it for future generations.

OPPOSITE **The Tank Museum's H3830 'on the open road'.**

ABOVE An armoured car crew in the Far East. H3830 was the original licence number of the Tank Museum's car, proving that it served in Shanghai with the 5th ACC between the wars. Notice the car in front, which has a ball mounting in the rear door for a Hotchkiss machine-gun.

The crew – roles and positions

During the period it was used by the Royal Tank Corps, the Rolls-Royce was operated by armoured car companies. As of December 1927 the War Establishment (full strength) of each company consisted of 14 officers and 160 men, plus a first reinforcement of 2 officers and 16 men who would not go with the company into action, but instead acted as an initial source of replacements for casualties. The company was divided into a headquarters and 4 sections each of 3 officers and 31 men.

Each company had a total of 17 armoured cars. Each section had 4, with the leftover car used by the company commander. The sections could be further split into sub-sections of two cars.

Each section also had two six-wheeled lorries and four motorcycles for support, and there were more lorries and motorcycles assigned to company headquarters.

The 1930 edition of *Crew Drill for Rolls-Royce Armoured Cars* detailed the roles and responsibilities of each crewman. According to this, the car was supposed to have a crew of four, although it was often operated with three or even two men, especially in the desert.

Crew commander

- He is responsible to his sub-section or section commander for the efficiency of the car, for the training and welfare of the crew, and that the crew and car are properly equipped.
- He supervises the duties of all other numbers of the crew, controls the car tactically and keeps in touch with his next superior commander.
- He is responsible for the stowing of the car.
- He is responsible for signal appliances and pyrenes (fire extinguishers).

No 1 – the driver

- He is responsible to the crew commander for the general mechanical efficiency and condition of his car, and that the petrol and oil tanks and radiator are filled before the car moves off.
- He will himself attend to the maintenance of the engine and transmission.
- He is responsible for the doors giving access to the engine, and the doors and loopholes used by himself when driving.

No 2 – the spare driver

- He assists No 1 as required.
- In inspections he is responsible for wheels, springs and all external parts of the car, also equipment.

No 3 – the gunner

- He is responsible for the gun and its spare parts and ammunition.

LEFT Crew commander. Putting H3830 through her paces at Tankfest 2016.

Steve Latham, former Royal Engineer and Centurion driver and Tank Museum volunteer

It is both a challenge and a privilege to be able to drive the Tank Museum's Rolls-Royce Silver Ghost armoured car, one of only two left of the 120 built. Driving on the road is a challenge. You need to be confident driving in modern-day traffic at a possible 45mph; you certainly get the feeling it will do much more. Keep in mind this is a 96-year-old car that requires respect.

It has a four-speed crash gearbox. The gearstick is on the right, next to the handbrake. You need to be prepared to change gear in advance as there is a holding notch at each gear position, so you must pull the stick out of the notch prior to moving into the next gear. The box is a crash box that must be double de-clutched up and down. I must admit this box is very smooth. (The commander may not think so.)

The car must be operated with two people as the driver has very limited vision through the visor with no view left or right, so you need a commander in the turret who can keep a watch out and give directions to other vehicles on the road. There are no indicators, so the commander gives hand signals, and no brake lights so he must also warn both the driver and vehicles close behind to keep back where

possible. Do not get too close to traffic lights – the driver cannot see them if he is too close.

The car has limited brakes on the rear wheels only. There is no power steering and it will not self-centre. It weighs 4.7 tonnes and there is hardly any suspension to smooth out the drain covers. If you hit one of these and you are not prepared then a severe steering wheel shudder sets in that is hard to control without stopping.

You must plan your trip with care, especially if it is a longer journey or one that might involve driving in darkness.

There are few lights; it does have headlights but no dip so you have a fixed illumination that has a yellow tinge. Drive within your limitations.

If you are going some distance, you will need to top up the engine with at least a pint of oil as the engine will use up oil . . . not because it is old . . . it's just the design which uses oil. You have no dipstick.

You will need to make a check on fuel – no dipstick or gauge again. Open the fuel tank filler and see how much is in there. A full tank will take you 150 miles with luck. It does about 6 to 7 miles to the gallon depending on the road conditions and traffic.

BELOW H3830 on country roads.

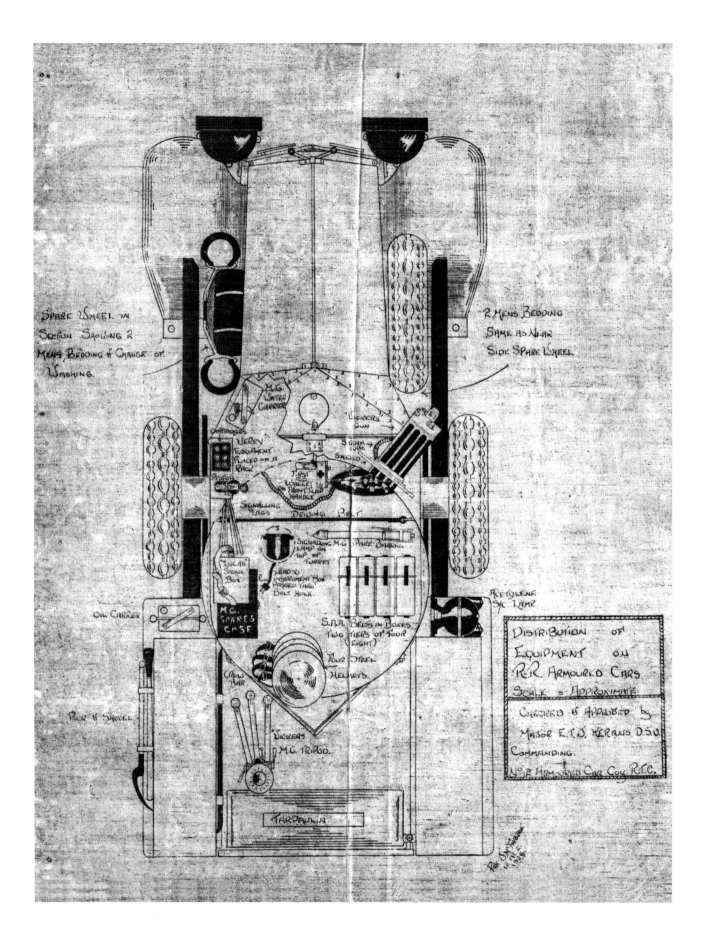

The crew's assigned positions depended on the circumstances. There were three states of readiness, 'Alert', 'Action' and 'March-at-ease'.

At 'Alert' and 'Action' the commander's place was in the turret, where he could best observe his surroundings. At 'March-at-ease' his position was seated on one of the toolboxes in the open rear compartment.

At 'Action' the No 3 manned the Vickers, with the commander positioned to his left. At 'Alert' and 'March-at-ease' he was seated on the floor of the car. He did not have a seat, although he did have access to a loose cushion.

At 'Alert', 'Action' and 'March-at-ease' crewman No 1 was to be at the wheel, with the No 2 next to him. Most cars gave the No 1 an adjustable seat, with the No 2 sitting on a cushion and supported by a slung webbing backrest. In 1920-pattern cars in Europe, however, they shared one cushion but had their own webbing backrests.

Equipment and stowage

Each car carried a defined list of equipment and spares to allow them and their crews to operate effectively. To ensure everything would fit, each item was to be positioned in a particular place, and the crews were issued with stowage diagrams to ensure standardisation.

Perhaps the most important equipment was .303 ammunition for the Vickers machine-gun. This was supplied in metal boxes that each contained a 250-round webbing belt. The 1920-pattern car carried nine boxes for a total of 2,250 rounds. The 1924-pattern carried 12, or 3,000 rounds, as well as two boxes containing 600 rounds in 50-round belts for the Hotchkiss machine-gun. The Vickers was also provided with a spare barrel and parts, as well as a tripod so that it could be used outside the car.

Two spare wheels were carried, one on each side. Stowed in the space behind each was bedding and spare clothing for two men. The crew's steel helmets were carried inside the car. On the 1924-pattern cars the crew was provided with an 18-pint (10.2l) drinking water tank. This was located in the passenger side toolbox on the rear platform, with a tap that could be accessed from inside.

Smaller tools and spare parts were carried in the toolboxes to the rear of the car, with larger items secured outside. Four pyrene fire extinguishers were positioned around the car 'in brackets which are readily accessible'.

Signalling equipment included flags, a Lucas signalling lamp and coloured cartridges for the Very flare pistol. There was no wireless. Semaphore, using the flags, was effective over short distances, and was generally used by crew commanders to signal between the cars in a unit. The Lucas signalling lamp, which used Morse code, had a much longer range. It could be removed from the car and mounted on a tripod, or, by opening the turret hatch, mounted on the roof (1924-pattern cars had a mounting inside the cupola). The Very pistol was handheld and used to fire flare cartridges in combinations of different colours. These combinations all had specific meanings.

In addition, each armoured car section had four motorcyclists who could be used as despatch riders to pass messages.

Procedures and drills

All aspects of operating the Rolls-Royce were carried out according to established drills. These ensured every crewman knew his precise role under all circumstances and that men could move from unit to unit without having to waste time learning a different way of accomplishing the same thing.

Gun drill

Loading, aiming and firing the machine-gun was carried out by the No 3 – the gunner – at the direction of the commander. He selected the target and controlled when the gunner would start and stop firing. The turret could traverse through 360 degrees. The mounting on 1924- and Mark 1A 1920-pattern cars could be elevated to 40 degrees and depressed to 15.

In 'March-at-ease' or 'Alert' state, the gun was clamped in place and unloaded. Only when the commander ordered 'Action' and the gunner took his place at the gun, would he load a belt and chamber a round.

When he had chosen a target the commander (C) would 'talk-on' the gunner (G). He would first give a bearing, then the range, then describe the target. At each stage the

OPPOSITE **This beautiful drawing on linen, which shows the stowage arrangement for equipment on a Rolls-Royce, was made by Private J.C. McFarlane of the 12th ACC and approved by his commanding officer, Major E.T.J. Kerans DSO in 1926.** *(E2012.2047)*

gunner would repeat the order before following it. An example would be:

C: 'Action.'
G: *Stands up, unclamps and loads gun and takes position behind it.*
C: 'Three o'clock.'
G: 'Three o'clock.' *Traverses turret to three o'clock position.*
C: 'Four hundred.'
G: 'Four hundred.' *Sets sights and picks an area at what he judges to be the correct range.*
C: 'Infantry.'
G: 'Infantry.' *Attempts to identify the target. Once he has, reports:*
G: 'On!'
C: 'Fire!'

The gunner would continue to fire on this target until ordered otherwise. He would fire in bursts of around 2–3 seconds, occasionally checking his aim between bursts. It is his responsibility to reload the gun and clear any stoppages as necessary.

The commander can order 'Stop!' to tell the gunner to stop firing, but maintain his aim on the target. If he orders 'Go on', the gunner will resume firing on that target, or alternatively the commander can assign a new one.

When the target has been destroyed the commander can either order 'Unload' to order the gunner to unload the gun, but remain ready, or 'Cease firing' to order him to unload, traverse the turret back to the front and clamp the gun in place.

Visor control

The armoured visor can be opened and closed by the driver [1]. The control lever has a number of notches cut into it that engage with a hold above the dashboard allowing it to be opened to different angles. The lever must always be secured in place with a split pin [2].

Radiator cover

The car's radiator plays a vital role in keeping the engine cool. However, it is vulnerable to damage if the car comes under fire [3]. For this reason the driver is provided with a lever allowing him to quickly close the armoured radiator cover from his seat. This protects the radiator, but makes it far less effective.

Running board drill

A less common operation was 'running board

drill'. Underneath the running boards are two ditching beams that can be detached and used as a bridge to allow the car to pass over obstacles [4]. Each is 8ft 3in (2.5m) long. They rest on small shelves and are held in place under the pressure of a large bolt [5]. To remove the beams the bolt is loosened, but not removed [6]. (The bolt is a modern replacement, originally a large wingnut was used, which could probably be loosened by hand.) The beams are then lifted out and positioned over the obstacle [7] [8]. According to the *Instruction Book*, this 'running board drill' was job for the whole crew, with the No 1 driving, No 2 and No 3 each assigned to a beam and the crew commander assisting each in turn and deciding on the beam's location.

Inspection and maintenance procedures

These procedures are used by Tank Museum staff to operate our Rolls-Royce armoured car. They generally follow the *Instruction Book* as used by Tank Corps soldiers during the 1920s and 1930s, but over the years some have been changed and adapted for the museum's needs.

Oiling the clutch

According to the *Instruction Book*, the clutch was to be oiled every 250 miles. To access it the small board next to the pedals is unlatched and removed **[1]**. This exposes the clutch **[2]**.

The clutch contains a cloth which must be kept lubricated. This is done by inserting the nozzle of the oil can into the top and bottom holes only **[3]**. It is important not to add too much oil, a few squirts of the can's thumb plunger are enough to lubricate the cloth.

Gearbox inspection and oiling

To access the gearbox the large floor panel should be removed **[4] [5]**. This gives access to the top of the gearbox, complete with prominent branding **[6]**. To check the oil the entire top, secured by nine bolts, is removed. The gearbox takes the form of an oil bath which should be roughly half-filled with oil. Overfilling it can blow the seals.

Lubricating the steering box

Correctly lubricating the Rolls-Royce was a vital part of keeping it running smoothly. A detailed chart was included in the *Instruction Book* showing each point and how often it should be lubricated. There are a large number of lubrication points – 26 on the prop shaft and suspension alone. Each linkage on these either has a grease nipple or needs to be oiled by hand using the can.

This is the lubrication point for the steering box [1], showing the grease nipple and the grease gun nozzle attached to it [2].

Exhaust cut-out

This pedal, operated by the driver's foot, operates a rocking lever that diverts the exhaust gases out before they reach the baffles in the exhaust silencer. In theory this was supposed to give the engine more power, although the team that restored *Sliabh na mBan* 'never found any perceivable improvement in power' when using it [3] [4].

However, there is no question that it makes the engine much louder, so understandably it is labelled 'Not for use in the United Kingdom'. [5] Among some Tank Museum staff it is also rumoured that it was used as a non-lethal way to try to scare away crowds.

127

DRIVING AND MAINTENANCE: OPERATING THE ROLLS-ROYCE ARMOURED CAR

Engine oil check and top-up

The Rolls-Royce pre-dates the widespread use of the oil dipstick, so checking the engine oil level is quite a complicated process. Outside on the passenger side of the car, just above the running board is the crankcase oil drain [1]. This lever is secured with a wingnut, which has to be removed [2]. The lever is then pulled away from the body of the car and rotated to the 'Open' position [3]. This opens the overflow cock underneath the car [4]. A thin, continuous stream shows the oil level is sufficient.

If the oil needs topping up, the oil filling plug [5] at the back of the engine compartment on the driver's side should be opened and filled [6].

Top-up oil in distributor driveshaft

The distributor driveshaft is driven from the camshaft. It rotates, using a trembler coil, to pass an electrical spark to the spark plugs in sequence as the engine runs. As a moving part it requires lubrication with oil. This is done via the small nozzle located in front of the distributor [7].

Radiator top-up

To top up the water in the radiator, the cap is first loosened with a spanner [1], then removed by hand [2]. The system holds 9 gallons of water.

Starting the engine

It is first necessary to ensure the car is fuelled. This is done by removing the wooden floor panel in the open rear of the car to expose the tank, then removing the nut on the tank to check the level.

The four-way cock is located on the passenger side of the car, just above the running boards. This must be set to 'Both Pumps' [1].

The fuel priming tap located on the engine bulkhead underneath the dashboard must be set to 'Running' [2]. The hand pump is then pumped until 2psi is shown on the fuel pressure gauge [3] [4]. The priming tap on the engine bulkhead is then set to 'Priming' and the hand pump operated five more times before the tap is set back to 'Running'.

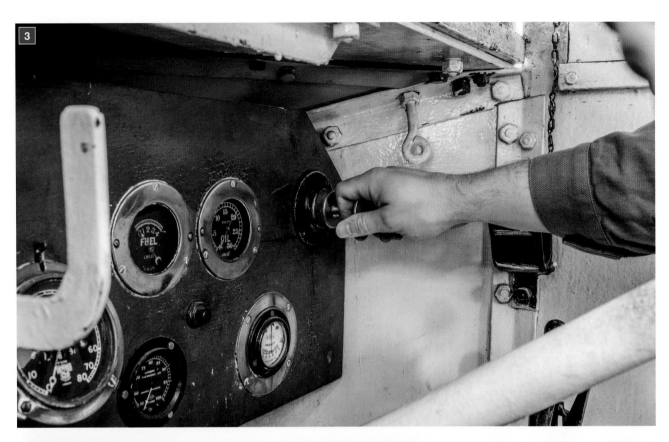

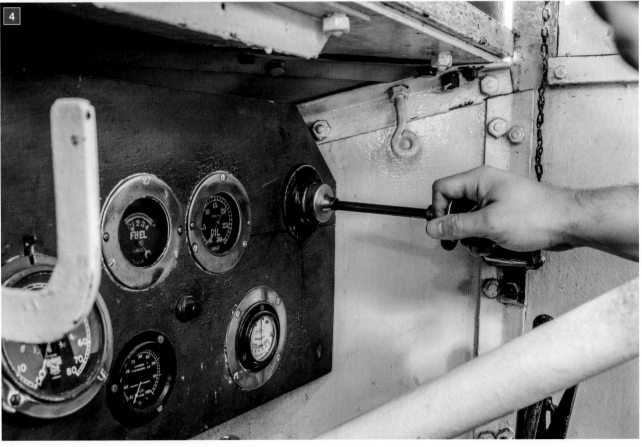

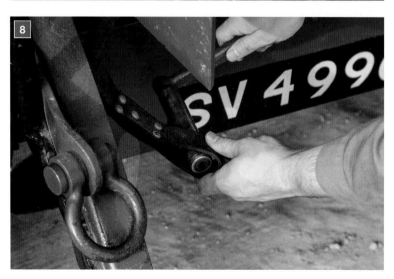

A modern addition to the start-up procedure is to turn on the isolator to activate electrical power.

The controls on the steering wheel must then be set correctly [5]. The central brass knob should be set to 'M & B' (magneto and battery) to use both electrical starters. Both governor and ignition levers are set at three-quarters of the way to the top (museum staff use the aide-memoire '10 to 2'). The conical brass carburation lever should be set to vertical, unless it is particularly cold, in which case it should be set to 'Strong'.

The gear lever must be in neutral and the handbrake set [6]. The clutch needs to be fully engaged [7]. The starter button (seen here above the driver's toe) can then be pressed with the left foot. The engine should start first time.

If the electric start fails at this point it is possible to start the engine using the starting handle.

To do this crewman No 2 should be positioned in front of the handle, facing the vehicle. The handle should be removed from its leather holder [8]. It will rotate freely unless it is pushed in against the spring. Once it is, it takes much more effort to rotate. The handle is turned clockwise. The upwards thrust is the most important, and as long as this is fast and powerful enough, the engine should start with one rotation [9].

Unlike in the photograph, do not wrap your thumb around the handle. If the engine kicks back this will drive the handle anti-clockwise, which could break your thumb.

The oil pressure should quickly rise to around 15psi and the ammeter should show 'Charge'. The engine must be warmed up before the car is driven.

If the fuel pressure begins to drop quickly, this suggests there is a leak in the system.

If the car runs badly, the priming tap may have been left on 'Priming'. If it has, the driver can switch it over to 'Running' with his foot. This can be done with the engine running.

Adjusting the fan belt

The fan belt must be kept taut. It can be adjusted by moving the lever in the centre of the fan spindle [10]. This is loosened by turning it anti-clockwise with a spanner. Once slackened, it can be moved up or down as necessary to tighten or slacken the belt. If the belt can be run backwards, it is too slack. The belt is driven by an excentric cam, so unless the lever is held securely while it is retightened, the belt will slip back.

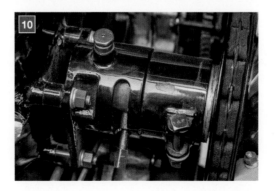

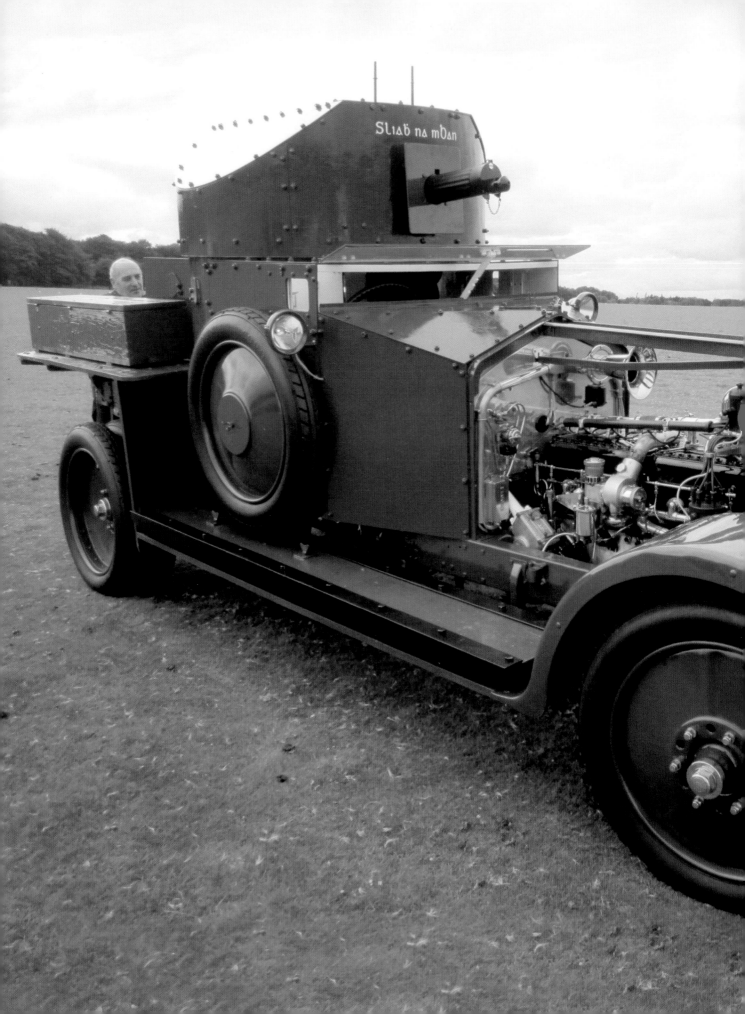

Chapter Seven

Restoring *Sliabh na mBan*

────────●────────

Captain Stephen Mac Eoin and James Black

'I drove Sliabh na mBan *all over the country, from country fairs to ceremonial events. It was always the centre of attention. Everyone wanted to be near a piece of history so closely connected with Michael Collins.'*

Pat Lynch, Foreman, Cavalry Workshops, 1970s

OPPOSITE *Sliabh na Mban* fully restored by James Black Restorations Ltd at Lisburn, Co Down. *(James Black Restorations)*

The history of
Sliabh na mBan

Captain Stephen Mac Eoin

The Rolls-Royce armoured car *Sliabh na mBan* occupies a special place in Irish military history and in the history of the Irish Defence Forces. *Sliabh na mBan* has seen service through three wars with three different armies and serves to illustrate, in a very visual way, a proud military tradition which is upheld to this day by the Cavalry Corps of the Defence Forces.

Sliabh na mBan, referred to as *Slievenamon* in its earlier, anglicised form, is one of 13 1920-pattern armoured Rolls-Royce cars (or ARR – as they are defined by the Irish military) which were acquired from the British by the Irish Free State after the Anglo-Irish Treaty of December 1921.

The Rolls-Royce armoured cars were deployed in Ireland, in the same theatre as the Peerless and Lancia armoured cars, but were seen as having the edge in terms of mobility, their slimline design later earning them the nickname 'the Whippet' in Ireland.

With the outbreak of Irish Civil War hostilities in June 1922 following bitter disagreement over the Anglo-Irish Treaty, the National Army (known from October 1924 as the Defence Forces), procured several key items of ordnance and equipment from the departing British. This included field artillery pieces and armoured vehicles, among them the 13 armoured Rolls-Royce (ARR) cars. There was originally some resistance from the British War Office to the provision of any *matériel* other than that which was freely available from surplus stocks built up during the First World War, such as rifles and lorries. Armoured Rolls-Royce cars had been provided to the Free State in an ad hoc manner as early as March 1922, but a long telegram from the Duke of Devonshire at the War Office to the Governor General of the Free State, dated 6 December 1922 (exactly a year to the day after the signing of the treaty) states, 'Under no conditions can [we] hand over any [further] Rolls-Royce armoured cars because they cannot be replaced here within many months, but . . . six Peerless armoured cars are at the disposal of your Government in Dublin. . . .' The telegram points to the value placed on the Rolls-Royce vehicles by the British themselves. However, once clear financial procedures had been put in place for the procurement of ordnance and equipment, 13 Rolls-Royce armoured cars in total were eventually handed over.

These vehicles were numbered ARR 1 to 14 (there was no ARR 13), and were eventually given nicknames such as *High Chief* (ARR 14), *Tom Keogh* (ARR 1) and of course *Slievenamon/Sliabh na mBan* (ARR 2). The anglicised version *Slievenamon* appears in the early period, due to the lack of formal standardisation in the spelling of words in the Irish language at that time, especially the early use of 'v' instead of the later 'bh'. Sliabh na mBan, incidentally, is the name of a mountain in Tipperary, the literal translation of which is 'Mountain of the Women', and it was the scene of a battle during the 1798 Rebellion. It is also

BELOW General Michael Collins (left) Commander-in-Chief of the Irish Free State Army who was ambushed and shot dead on 22 August 1922. He is pictured with General Richard Mulcahy, his Chief of Staff. *(Topham Picturepoint)*

LEFT This is probably the last picture of Michael Collins, seated in the back of his yellow Leyland open touring car with Major-General Emmet Dalton, taken outside the Lees Hotel, Bandon, on 22 August 1922. *(TopFoto)*

the name of a popular Tipperary folk ballad. To confuse matters further, the vehicles were later given standard Irish registration plate numbers; ARR 2 becoming YI 6450.

What has assured *Sliabh na mBan*'s special place in history is the fact that it formed part of General Michael Collins' convoy which was ambushed on 22 August 1922 at Béal na mBláth in West Cork. The ambush resulted in the tragic death of General Collins, who was then Commander-in-Chief of the National Army (with General Richard Mulcahy as Chief of Staff).

General Collins had left from GHQ at Portobello (now Cathal Brugha) Barracks in Rathmines, Dublin, to inspect his troops in the Southern (later Cork) Command who were fighting against Anti-Treaty forces in the Civil War. Despite strong advice not to venture into what was effectively a heartland of the Anti-Treaty side – including advice from Joe McGrath, Director of Intelligence – General Collins insisted on touring through West Cork, apparently with the intention of seeking a meeting with some of the Anti-Treaty leaders, including Liam Lynch, to broker a peace agreement. The convoy included Collins' touring car, a Crossley tender lorry, a motorbike outrider and of course *Sliabh na mBan*.

It appears that General Collins' convoy had passed through Béal na mBláth earlier that day on its route from Macroom to Bandon.

They had been observed by a group of officers from the Cork No 3 Brigade of the Anti-Treaty forces, who decided to set up an ambush in case the convoy returned. Owing to the widespread destruction of communications such as roads and bridges in the area, Collins travelled from Bandon through Clonakilty and then from Rosscarberry back through Béal na mBláth. The convoy was ambushed late in the evening of 22 August 1922, as light was beginning to fade. Crucially, the decision was taken – possibly by Collins – to dismount and return fire rather than drive through the ambush as standard anti-ambush drills would dictate. The Vickers machine-gun in the turret of *Sliabh na mBan*, having fired perhaps 200 rounds at the Anti-Treaty positions, may have jammed during the ambush – a feature which is not uncommon for machine-guns and in this case depended largely on correct feeding of the cloth ammunition belt for the Vickers gun. Other accounts state that a problem may have developed with the gas regulation in the Vickers toggle-lock action, resulting in the machine-gun firing irregular single shots rather than automatic fire. Controversy later arose when the gunner in the car, 'Jock' McPeake, a former soldier in the British Army, defected to the Anti-Treaty side with *Sliabh na mBan*, some months later. The car was subsequently recovered by Free State forces in December 1922.

While historians differ in opinion over what exactly happened at Béal na mBláth, most are in agreement that General Collins was shot once in the head, possibly from a richochet, in open ground on the roadway while returning fire and away from the safety that the armour might have afforded him. Major-General Emmet Dalton took Collins' body into *Sliabh na mBan* and the convoy escaped the ambush with no other casualties. General Collins was brought to Shanakiel Hospital in Cork later that night.

When news of the tragedy reached Army GHQ early in the morning on 23 August, General Mulcahy, who was to succeed General Collins, famously issued his message of restraint 'to the men of the Army' and urged soldiers of the National Army to 'let no cruel act of reprisal blemish your bright honour'. General Mulcahy's message concluded with the cry 'Ireland! The Army serves, strengthened by its sorrow.'

Sliabh na mBan went on to serve in the Cork Command for the remainder of the Civil War and was absorbed into the newly formed Armoured Car Corps in 1923. Interestingly, one ARR was stationed as part of the military guard at Government Buildings during the Civil War, and a note from Army GHQ to the Minister for Defence in September 1923 points out that '. . . parts of the car are being destroyed with rust . . .' (due to constant service outside in the elements, without shelter) and that '. . . the need for maintaining this car at Government Buildings would seem to have passed . . .'.

Following the end of the Civil War in May 1923, the Army was downsized by approximately 30,000 personnel and further contractions into the 1930s resulted in the ARRs remaining together as the only armoured car squadron in the newly formed Cavalry Corps. By 1936, the ageing ARRs were superseded by Landsverk 180 armoured cars, and departmental files from the late 1930s point to difficulties in terms of procurement of spare parts for repairs and in the availability of finance in the Defence Vote. However, the ARRs, including *Sliabh na mBan*, were returned to full service as the 2nd Armoured Car Squadron from late 1939, by which stage imported armoured vehicles were almost impossible to procure due to the conflict in Europe. Records show that the Defence Forces acquired two

civilian Rolls-Royce limousines in 1940 as a source of spare parts. In order to augment the ARR and Landsverk armoured cars, the Armoured Fighting Vehicle Construction and Design Board had been established. This board had been set up as early as January 1933 under Major A. Lawlor, and also resulted in the production of the Leyland armoured car.

The Second World War, known as 'The Emergency' in Ireland, prompted the development of other Irish-made armoured fighting vehicles – including notably the Ford armoured car. The Ford was manufactured from a Ford lorry chassis (there was a Ford plant in Cork at the time) and a steel plate hull from Thompson's of Carlow after a design by Colonel J.V. Lawless, a Cavalry Corps officer who had served on the 1933 Board. These vehicles then formed the 2nd Armoured Car Squadron during the Emergency (the ARRs were redesignated as the 3rd Armoured Car Squadron). Interestingly, a decision was later taken to retrofit the ARRs with the same commander's cupola and gun ball mounting as that designed for the Ford Mark VI. Meanwhile, Ireland's small peacetime army had been expanded to include, at maximum strength, 41,000 personnel, with 106,000 reservists in the Local Defence Force. It is worth noting that the British Army was also still using the 1920-pattern ARRs (with some modifications) during the Second World War, notably in Iraq in the summer of 1941. The Ford (Mark VI) would go on to provide light armoured support for Irish Defence Forces personnel in the early battalion deployments on peacekeeping duties overseas with ONUC (Congo) in the early 1960s, still carrying the Vickers .303in machine-gun.

By March 1947, the Defence Forces had been reduced to a strength of 8,803 personnel and there was no longer a place for the ARRs in the peacetime army. They were quietly retired in The Curragh Camp, where unofficial efforts to preserve *Sliabh na mBan* ensured its survival during the lean years of the late 1940s and early 1950s. Records at military archives show that on 28 April 1954, 12 of the ARRs (minus their turrets and armoured plate) were publicly auctioned at McKee Barracks, fetching values of between £27 and £60. However, the Secretary of the Department of Defence, in a letter to the Minister of Finance dated 26 March 1954, mentions the preservation of one Rolls-Royce armoured car as a museum piece in the Cavalry Workshops, as well as another of the ARR engines for instructional purposes in the Cavalry Depot. Accordingly, the Rolls-Royce vehicle YI 6450 – which is ARR 2, *Sliabh na mBan* – does not appear on the auction list for that day.

The expertise of military and civilian personnel at the Cavalry Workshops since the 1950s has ensured the survival of *Sliabh na mBan* as a unique piece of Irish military heritage. *Sliabh na mBan* retains its historical pride of place as the oldest Cavalry Corps vehicle and one which now remains in perfect working order following extensive refurbishment in the summer of 2011, under careful supervision of the Defence Forces' Combined Vehicle Base Workshops.

Sliabh na mBan will soon celebrate her 100th birthday, by which stage her famous Rolls-Royce engine will of course have only just been broken in. . . .

Restoring *Sliabh na mBan*

James Black, James Black Restorations Ltd, Lisburn, Northern Ireland

We were delighted to receive a request from the Irish Army to complete a short feasibility study on the restoration of the Rolls-Royce armoured car in their possession. After this was completed we were eventually requested to restore the vehicle with assistance from Irish Army personnel.

Sliabh na mBan was preserved as a curiosity by sympathetic staff at The Curragh Cavalry workshops at Co. Kildare and was eventually recognised as the undoubted national treasure it is.

We were delighted to be appointed to be involved in the restoration of this fascinating and historic vehicle. Our first task was to accurately photograph and make drawings of all the component parts prior to dismantling. During this procedure we found that although

BELOW *Sliabh na Mban* **pre-restoration.**

the cavalry mechanics had done their best with the parts and tools available, the vehicle was in pretty poor condition with a lot of wear on the chassis, shackle pins, bushes, etc., and had a major break in the back axle assembly (torque tube).

The engine was only running on three cylinders and needed a major overhaul with compressions on all cylinders being very poor. The radiator was almost entirely blocked, but the chassis frame itself was in good condition. The armoured body, although scruffy, was in excellent condition. The Vickers machine-gun had been deactivated and only required refurbishment. The original dash had been removed and replaced with a rough piece of timber.

ABOVE The unrestored rear axle showing the twin wheels. This arrangement is only found on the armoured chassis.

RIGHT The restored rear axle and torque tube.

RIGHT The restored rear axle.

ABOVE Fitting the brake ropes.

LEFT Detail of rear of the chassis showing the extra cross member to add strength due to the heavier springs. This was not found on the standard chassis.

ABOVE Rear spring with 15 leaves to carry the armoured body. The civilian car typically had 9 or 10 leaves.

ABOVE RIGHT Interior showing the auxiliary starting cog and shaft used to start the car from inside if the electric starter failed while in action.

RIGHT The unrestored car during dismantling.

FAR LEFT Each piece of armour is marked with an individual number.

LEFT The armoured radiator covers.

BELOW Engine prior to restoration.

ABOVE LEFT Oil pump dismantled.

ABOVE Distributor showing position of the air pump. This pump provided air for the fuel system. The cylinder has been removed to show the piston of the compressor.

LEFT The restored starter motor.

BELOW The restored engine before being fitted to the chassis.

We commenced the dismantling, cataloguing and cleaning of parts while the body and chassis remained at The Curragh and the excellent team at the workshops proceeded to dismantle the body and prepare for painting. We removed the front and back axle and engine and brought them to our Lisburn workshop.

The engine was a relatively straightforward job; we have completed many Silver Ghost engines, so we had no surprises. The back axle, however, created all sorts of difficulties as the torque tube had snapped completely in two, the consequence I believe of some very hard and harsh driving. The net result of this was that the crown wheel and pinion and bearing were completely mashed. Replacement components were sought and acquired and the back axle rebuilt. The front axle was comprehensively overhauled including king pins, bearings, etc., and the three components front and back axle and engine were delivered back to The Curragh.

Our next task was to restore the bulkhead, steering column and gearbox; this work took another two months. Our last job was the restoration of the chassis frame itself; this again was completed at our workshops in Lisburn, where it was painted Irish Army regulation battleship grey.

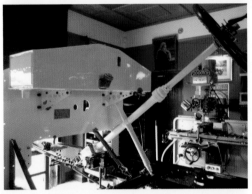

ABOVE The restored front axle with wheels removed.

LEFT Restored bulkhead showing the reserve oil and petrol tank unique to Rolls-Royce armoured cars and not fitted to the standard car.

LEFT Front bulkhead showing the Rolls-Royce chassis plate and electric starter button.

In the meantime the staff at The Curragh had beautifully repainted the outside of the hull and turret. They also painted the inside white, which would be correct for the period; however, after our exhaustive research and a visit to the Tank Museum at Bovington to inspect the British Rolls-Royce armoured car, we came to the conclusion that it needed to be a more subtle tone of white, which was subsequently applied.

The reassembly of *Sliabh na mBan* took approximately six weeks and necessitated myself and Colin Bell, my chief engineer, spending two to three days a week in the workshops at The Curragh. Myself and Colin had the assistance of four or five very able men of the Irish Army maintenance workshop. The vehicle had to be completed for the Irish Army

ABOVE Unrestored gearbox.

RIGHT Chassis being dismantled.

RIGHT Chassis under restoration.

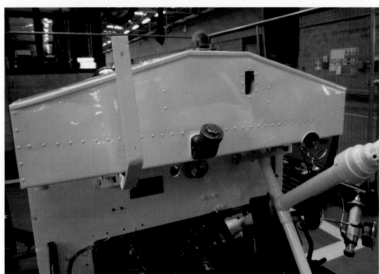

TOP The shot-blasted chassis, showing towing brackets front and rear, and the extra cross member at the rear for strength. Also visible is the under-chassis bracing common to all Silver Ghost chassis built after 1911.

ABOVE The restored gear change and handbrake quadrant.

ABOVE RIGHT Reserve oil and petrol tank showing the slot for the radiator cover lever.

RIGHT Restored hull fitted to chassis.

RIGHT A test-drive without radiator armour.

RIGHT The finished article.

RIGHT First test-firing of the Vickers gun.

Cavalry Day on 3 September 2011 and we are very glad to say we met our deadline.

After assembly, the vehicle started first time and with very little work to carburation and it ran and drove as it should. I have driven the vehicle myself at 40mph across the grassy plains surrounding The Curragh and she managed 66mph on the open road, which isn't bad for an armoured vehicle fitted with low-ratio gearing. The vehicle was presented to the An Taoiseach Enda Kelly TD, where he commended us on our work. We as a company were honoured and delighted to have been offered the opportunity to work on this iconic Rolls-Royce as there are only two or three surviving examples, and having inspected them I have no hesitation in saying that *Sliabh na mBan* is probably the best example of its type in the world.

BELOW The Irish Army sent *Sliabh na mBan* to the 2013 Tankfest event at Bovington.

Appendix

Preserved Rolls-Royce armoured cars

BELOW This is the oldest of them all: chassis No 21GB saw service in the First World War before going to India. It can be seen in the Indian Cavalry Tank Museum at Ahmednagar.

'It is customary to comment on historic vehicle values, even when they are not for sale, and never will be: there's only one such other in working condition in Dublin. . . . All the other survivors were deliberately broken up . . . I'd say . . . er, ho hum . . . six million quid? Probably.'

Tony Dron, *Daily Telegraph Motoring Review*, **2 August 1997**

The oldest preserved armoured Rolls-Royce of all is a 1914-pattern turreted armoured car, chassis number 21GB (the chassis number was identified by John Fasal). This would have been one of the original Royal Naval Armoured Car Division vehicles, later transferred to the War Office, but whether it was one of the original six sent from London to India or whether it was one of the eight cars serving with 13th Light Armoured Motor Battery in Persia, which were transferred to India when 13th LAMB was disbanded, we simply don't know. In India it would have served with 7th Armoured Car Company, Royal Tank Corps, which arrived there on 15 February 1921. It has two features typical of Rolls-Royces in India – the narrow steel disc wheels and Macintosh normal air pressure tyres (which in fact were semi-solids) and two loopholes with armoured covers in each of the turret bevels intended for firing rifles through at snipers on the mountainsides of the North-West Frontier. The car, which is now in rather a dilapidated state, is displayed at the Indian Cavalry Tank Museum at Ahmednagar, Maharashtra, India.

There are effectively three Irish Rolls-Royce armoured cars, or at least their chassis, in preservation. No 103 WO is preserved complete by the Irish Defence Forces Cavalry Corps at The Curragh Camp. The car is still generally known as *Slievenamon* in Hiberno-English, but its proper Gaelic name is *Sliabh na mBan*. It is said to be the car that was escorting General Michael Collins, who was both Chairman of the Provisional Government and Commander-in-Chief of the Irish National Army, when he was shot and killed at Beál na mBláth in August 1922 during the Irish Civil War. The car was fully restored to original condition by James Black Restorations Ltd, Lisburn, Northern Ireland.

The chassis of Rolls-Royce armoured car 161 WO is preserved and displayed at Cité de l'Automobile Musée, originally known as the Schlumpf Collection, at Mulhouse in France. In Irish service, 161 WO was known as ARR 6 *Custom House*. The other surviving chassis

BELOW The Irish Army's exquisitely restored Rolls-Royce, 103WO *Sliabh na mBan*. It is believed to be the car that was escorting Michael Collins when he was killed in August 1922.

LEFT *Tom Keogh* was an Irish Army armoured car. A replica body has since been rebuilt on the original chassis, 101 WO, and is in private hands.

is 101 WO, which was probably from the first 1920-pattern car ever built. It is now running under a replica aluminium body (instead of the original armoured steel) as ARR1 *Tom Keogh*, named after the Irish Colonel-Commandant who was killed in a mine explosion at Macroom in September 1922. Originally the car was known as *Danny Boy*. In its replica guise the car was built and is owned by Mr John Malamatenios of Hertfordshire.

BELOW The Tank Museum's 1920-pattern car F247 (H3830). Notice that on these cars the two vision slits in the visor are at different heights.

The 1920-pattern armoured car preserved at the Tank Museum at Bovington in Dorset is F247. Originally it had the Middlesex registration number H3830. Although this was later changed it is still running on chassis number 193 WO. It was originally issued to 5th Armoured Car Company, Tank Corps (later Royal Tank Corps), when that was based in Dublin. It was created on 29 May 1920 from the old 17th (Armoured Car) Battalion, Tank Corps, when that was disbanded. The 5th Armoured Car Company then went to Belfast and from there, on 14 March 1923, to Scarborough.

On 29 January 1927 it sailed for Shanghai, taking its cars with it. On 16 February 1929 it landed at Port Said on the way back from Shanghai. Later on, the men formed 6th Tank Battalion and handed their armoured cars over to the 12th Royal Lancers who had just mechanised. The 11th Hussars arrived in Egypt on 25 November 1934 to change stations with the 12th Royal Lancers and also took over their armoured cars. The older cars were steadily being replaced by newer ones and, although the regiment was sent on internal security duties to Palestine in 1936, we cannot be sure whether F247 was with them or not. However, we suspect it was back in Britain by 1939 although we can't say exactly what it was doing.

It came to the Tank Museum in about 1947 although it has the accession number E1949.329. In May 1997 it was used to provide transport for Her Majesty Queen Elizabeth II when she visited the Tank Museum, and is kept in good running order. It is maintained in excellent condition and is original, apart from the driver's seat. A proper one has been fitted in place of the cushion on the floor and the leather backrest as seen on the original cars.

Bibliography and sources

Anon, *Rolls-Royce and the Great Victory* (Bronte-Hill Publications, 1972)

Bird, Anthony and Hallows, Ian, *The Rolls-Royce Motor Car* (Batsford, 1984)

Dun, Major T.I., *From Cairo to Siwa Across the Libyan Desert with Armoured Cars* (E. & R. Schindler, Cairo, 1933)

Fasal, John and Goodman, Bryan, *The Edwardian Rolls-Royce* (John Fasal, 1994)

Fletcher, David, *The Rolls-Royce Armoured Car* (Osprey Publishing, 2012)

Fletcher, David, *War Cars* (HMSO, 1987)

Kautt, W.H., *Ambushes and Armour, the Irish Rebellion 1919–1923* (Irish Academic Press, 2010)

Kutz, Captain C.R., *War on Wheels* (Military Service Publishing, 1940)

Martin, Karl, *Irish Army Vehicles* (Karl Martin, 2002)

Myers, A. Wallis, *Captain Anthony Wilding* (Hodder & Stoughton, 1917)

Raliegh, Walter, *War in the Air, Vol. 1* (Clarendon Press, 1922)

Rolls, S.C., *Steel Chariots in the Desert* Rolls-Royce Enthusiasts Club (1988)

Roosevelt, Kermit, *War in the Garden of Eden* (Charles Scribner, 1919)

Samson, Air Commodore Charles Rumney, *Fights and Flights* (Ernest Benn Ltd., 1930)

Sueter, Rear Admiral Sir Murray, *The Evolution of the Tank* (Hutchinson & Co., 1937)

Warwick, Nigel W.M., *In Every Place* (Forces & Corporate Publishing, 2014)

White, B.T., *British Tanks and Fighting Vehicles 1914–1945* (Ian Allan, 1970)

Whittall, W., *With Botha and Smuts in Africa* (Cassell, 1917)

Winstone, H.V.F., *Leachman, O.C. Desert* (Quarter Books, 1982)

Miscellaneous sources

Various volumes of *History of the Great War, Military Operations;* assorted regimental histories; the *Royal Tank Corps Journal* – various articles and extracts from different volumes; and manuals and other documents from the Tank Museum archives.

Index